STRATEGIC COST-CUTTING

How to Improve Profitability in a Downturn

JASON SCHENKER

STRATEGIC COST-CUTTING

How to Improve Profitability in a Downturn

BY JASON SCHENKER

ISBN: 978-1-946197-55-9 *Paperback*
978-1-946197-56-6 *Ebook*

PRESTIGE
PROFESSIONAL PUBLISHING

For business leaders trying to keep their companies afloat.

CONTENTS

CONTENTS

CONTENTS

STRATEGIC COST-CUTTING

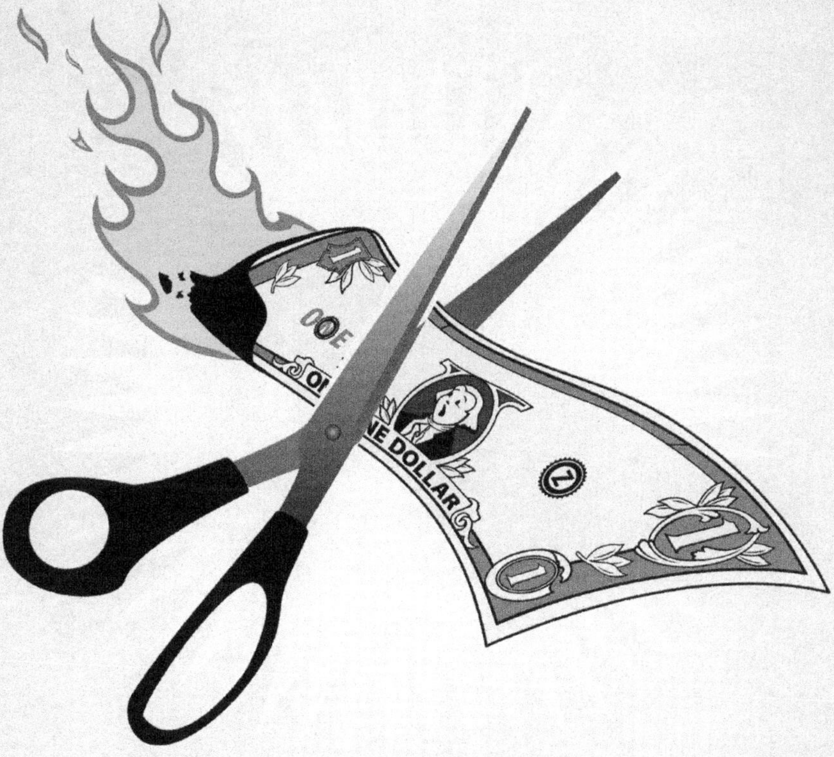

JASON SCHENKER

PREFACE

WRITING ABOUT STRATEGIC COST-CUTTING

Businesses preparing for an economic recovery will face challenges in the years ahead. And while they will need to cut costs, the right cuts will need to be strategic, to ensure the greatest long-term potential for business profitability and success.

In *Strategic Cost-Cutting,* I lay out a strategic plan to achieve success in challenging times. That is the big idea of this book: to help businesses take critical actions to ensure long-term success.

The impact of slower economic growth is likely to cast a shadow — in both bad and good ways — across the years and decades ahead. It will impact how we work, where we live, and what different industries will look like in the future. But in the short term, cutting costs will be critical for business survival and economic growth.

This book draws on research, courses, and training materials from The Futurist Institute's Certified Futurist program, as well as research from Prestige Economics.

Making Tough Decisions

This book represents an attempt to strategically approach the difficult issue of cutting costs. Of course, cutting some costs is easier than cutting others. After all, revisiting expenses that might be less than critical is very different than making difficult decisions about the labor market.

I have tried to write this book in a way that starts with some of the most critical basics and then goes on to more complicated strategies, ending with some of the most difficult decisions.

Acknowledgements

No book is done completely alone. There are editorial, file conversion, design, and project management parts of the project to get a book like this completed. And those tasks require a team.

Along those lines, I want to thank The Futurist Institute and Prestige Professional Publishing staff for making this book a reality. And I want to especially thank **Nawfal Patel**, who managed the production of *Strategic Cost-Cutting: How to Improve Profitability in a Downturn.* He did a tremendous job managing the team — and my own workflow.

I also want to thank **Kerry Ellis** for her fine work on the cover of this book. For this cover, I drew a very rough mock-up of the cover. And I do mean very rough. It was not very artistic in the least, but Kerry made the cover come to life.

Most importantly, I want to thank my family for supporting me in my education, career, entrepreneurship, and authorship.

I am always most grateful for the support of my loving wife, **Ashley Schenker**, and to my wonderful parents, **Janet and Jeffrey Schenker**.

My family supports me in countless ways by providing emotional support and editorial feedback. Every time I write a book, it's a crazy experience that spills over into my family life, so to them and to everyone else who helped me in this process: Thank you!

Finally, thank you for buying this book. I hope *Strategic Cost-Cutting* helps you and your business improve your profitability in these uncertain times!

~ Jason Schenker

OVERVIEW

INTRODUCTION

WHY I WROTE THIS BOOK

I wrote this book for my clients.

To help them during this difficult time — and the even more difficult times ahead.

But I also wrote this for all the other business leaders who will be forced to make difficult choices in the months and quarters ahead.

The recent business, economic, social, and public health challenges have been significant. There has been widespread disruption of the economy and businesses — as well as massive job losses. And the economic and business road to recovery may not be a quick and easy one.

Because 70 percent of the economy is driven by consumption, it has become very clear that a historic rise in the level of U.S. joblessness and the unemployment rate will have significantly negative impacts on businesses and the economy.

Many nonessential, nonremote service jobs are at risk — and they will be lost. And this could very likely be true beyond the immediate term.

Plus, credit is likely to be constricted in coming quarters, which presents additional business risks as well as risks to housing and the automotive industry.

I have written this book to help companies address the business and economic risks that likely lie ahead.

And the advice herein is also likely to be actionable following any other future potential economic conditions where there is a high level of risk to business profitability — and a need to cut costs.

To meet this end, I have divided this book into six sections:

— **Overview**
— **Spend Analysis**
— **Making Cuts**
— **Asset Recovery and Disposition**
— **Labor Cost-Cutting**
— **Forward-Looking Strategies**

In the **Overview** section of *Strategic Cost-Cutting*, I discuss the importance of strategic cost-cutting — rather than just haphazardly cutting costs.

I also discuss the biggest challenges in a downturn, business priorities in a downturn, and the importance of profitability. This section of the book helps the reader understand and describe the stakes and the battle plan to sustain company profitability.

In the second section of the book, **Spend Analysis**, I explain how to gather, clean, prioritize, and benchmark company expenses. I also discuss off-limits topics. This section of the book helps the reader understand the process to analyze company data, as well as how to implement the process in their own company.

Making Cuts is the focus of the third section of this book. This section of the book focuses on prioritizing vendors, negotiations, reverse auctions, exiting contracts, and reducing physical overhead. These may be difficult cuts to make, but they are an easier set of cuts than making labor cuts. This section of the book includes actionable strategies to cut costs. The reader will be able to take cost-cutting action after reading this section of the book.

In the fourth section of the book, **Asset Recovery and Disposition**, I explain the process of asset recovery, asset identification, asset redeployment and repurposing, and asset disposition and divestiture.

The focus of these strategies is to find ways to repurpose, reuse, or otherwise salvage company assets to help the business cut costs, maintain cash flow, and grow. The reader will be able to implement these strategies after reading this section.

Labor Cost-Cutting is the toughest cost-cutting topic. And it is the focus of fifth section of this book. This section includes a discussion of the most important company labor considerations, the first kind of labor cost cutting that comes from reducing overtime and contract labor.

The final part of this chapter includes a discussion of layoffs, which may be the last move almost any business leader wants to take to cut costs. After reading this section, the most important labor considerations, priorities, and process will be clear — even if the process will still be very difficult to implement.

The final section of this book focuses on **Forward-Looking Strategies**. This part of the book takes the optimistic look ahead at what actions can be taken to help ensure the greatest potential to capture upside beyond the economic downturn. This section includes two pieces of advice for business leaders who both own and run businesses: Hold on. And just don't get fired.

After reading through this section of the book, the reader will be able to frame the importance of looking beyond the downturn as well as plan for upside in the future. There is also a set of cost-cutting tables so that the reader can more effectively cut costs.

The goal of this book is to give the reader a toolkit to approach the challenging time ahead, to help business leaders keep their companies alive, and to prepare them for better times beyond the downturn.

Although the advice in this book is designed to be helpful, it is my hope that the strategies in this book will be able to help those who go through future economic downturns.

There's a reason why people call the dynamics of the economy a business cycle. It's because there are repeating patterns of growth and recession. And in future business cycles, there will again be a need to cut costs. But hopefully, if businesses remain vigilant with their expenses and spend, those businesses will be more profitable for longer — and they will be more resilient in downturns.

With all that in mind, let's get started!

After all, profitability isn't going to just improve itself.

CHAPTER 1

THE IMPORTANCE OF STRATEGIC COST-CUTTING

When the economy slows and recessions hit, strategic cost-cutting is critical.

It's not just enough to plan to cut costs when the going gets tough. Cuts have to be strategic — they need to be deliberate, intentional, and effective. And this is true when we consider the impact of cost-cutting during the downturn as well as the implications for during and after a recovery.

After all, it's important not to throw the baby out with the bathwater. And while some people plan to just cut, cut, cut their way to profitability, strategic cost-cutting offers much better long-term company benefits than just haphazardly cutting costs.

As you'll see in coming chapters there are a few concepts that you need to consider about costs:
— Is there low-hanging fruit worth grabbing for?
— Is enough value created by cutting certain costs?
— What will future costs be of any cuts?

There is no such thing as a free lunch, and every time costs are cut, there may be consequences. Cuts could adversely affect vendor relationships, staff morale, future competitiveness, and future readiness for recovery. This means that cuts in the present could reduce future long-term upside potential.

And that is something to avoid if possible.

In short, the best strategy when looking at cost-cutting, is to make sure that the juice is always worth the squeeze. Because each cut will come at a cost. And it's important that cuts aren't so deep that a company can't recover from them.

CHAPTER 2

THE BIGGEST CHALLENGES IN A DOWNTURN

Recessions have been traditionally defined by economists as two or more consecutive quarters of negative gross domestic product growth, otherwise known as GDP.

During those two or more quarters, the level of GDP falls. This doesn't mean that GDP as a sum of consumption, government spending, investment, and net exports is negative; it means that the level of growth declines, which makes the percent change from one quarter to the next quarter negative.

But the definition of recession changed after the 2001 recession, in which there was a quarter of negative growth followed by a quarter of positive growth, which was subsequently followed by a quarter of negative growth.

The National Bureau of Economic Research (NBER), which is a recognized authority on business cycle research in the United States, defines the timing of U.S. recessions.

Since 2010, the NBER has been using a slightly different definition of recession than the traditional definition involving two negative consecutive quarters of growth: "A recession is a significant decline in economic activity spread across the economy, lasting more than a few months, normally visible in real GDP, real income, employment, industrial production, and wholesale-retail sales."[1]

The NBER defines itself as "a private, non-profit, non-partisan organization dedicated to conducting economic research and to disseminating research findings among academics, public policy makers, and business professionals,"[2] according to the NBER website at www.nber.org.

Since the NBER definition of recession is good enough for the Fed, it's good enough for me! I have used the NBER dates and definition of recession throughout previous books.

A table of NBER recession dates is in Figure 2-1.

In all likelihood, the United States was already in a recession when this book went to print in April 2020. Although that recession may or may not meet the original historical definition of recession, it is almost certainly likely to meet the post-2010 definition of recession, regardless of GDP growth rates across multiple consecutive quarters. As such, the weakness in real income, employment, industrial production, and retail sales should be recognized as a threat to countless businesses.

Figure 2-1: Recession Dates According to the NBER[3]

BUSINESS CYCLE REFERENCE DATES

Quarterly dates are in parentheses

Peak	Trough
	December 1854 (IV)
June 1857(II)	December 1858 (IV)
October 1860(III)	June 1861 (III)
April 1865(I)	December 1867 (I)
June 1869(II)	December 1870 (IV)
October 1873(III)	March 1879 (I)
March 1882(I)	May 1885 (II)
March 1887(II)	April 1888 (I)
July 1890(III)	May 1891 (II)
January 1893(I)	June 1894 (II)
December 1895(IV)	June 1897 (II)
June 1899(III)	December 1900 (IV)
September 1902(IV)	August 1904 (III)
May 1907(II)	June 1908 (II)
January 1910(I)	January 1912 (IV)
January 1913(I)	December 1914 (IV)
August 1918(III)	March 1919 (I)
January 1920(I)	July 1921 (III)
May 1923(II)	July 1924 (III)
October 1926(III)	November 1927 (IV)
August 1929(III)	March 1933 (I)
May 1937(II)	June 1938 (II)
February 1945(I)	October 1945 (IV)
November 1948(IV)	October 1949 (IV)
July 1953(II)	May 1954 (II)
August 1957(III)	April 1958 (II)
April 1960(II)	February 1961 (I)
December 1969(IV)	November 1970 (IV)
November 1973(IV)	March 1975 (I)
January 1980(I)	July 1980 (III)
July 1981(III)	November 1982 (IV)
July 1990(III)	March 1991(I)
March 2001(I)	November 2001 (IV)
December 2007 (IV)	June 2009 (II)

As I discuss at length in the next chapter, the biggest challenges for businesses in a recession are to keep the cash flowing, remain profitable, and hold on to as many resources as possible to ensure upside during and after the economy recovers.

CHAPTER 3

BUSINESS PRIORITIES

Companies only go out of business for one reason: They run out of money. This is why maintaining positive cash flow and being able to service debt obligations is critical in a downturn.

Fortunately, the equation of profitability is always the same, in good times and bad: Revenue minus costs equals profits.

As such, there are only two ways to boost profits: sell more or spend less.

In good economic times, the focus is often on driving up revenue. And companies are sometimes willing to overlook costs while the money is flowing in.

Travel and entertainment expenses, maintenance expenses, equipment expenses, overtime hours, and other labor expenses can rise significantly as companies rush to capture the upside from increased sales.

As my colleague Nawfal Patel likes to say, "People are too busy making money to ask why or how."

However, during a recession or other economic or business slowdown, sales often fall. Sometimes sales stall altogether, as they did for many companies at the time this book was published.

Since increasing sales is tough — but cash flow and profitability are critical — business leaders will often turn their focus on cost cutting, as the only other way to support profitability.

Of course, this is very tough for some companies.

After all, high-growth companies — especially startups — often prioritize growth over profits. But these companies will face even greater challenges in a downturn, when sales fall and investor dollars could dry up quickly.

Such companies would need to find a way to become profitable after only ever having lost money. That could prove a tall task.

But these companies are the exception, not the rule.

Fortunately, most companies survive day to day in good times and bad because they are generally profitable. And they do not show constant negative earnings living only on investor support.

The good news is that for the great majority of companies that usually show profits, it's a lot easier to keep the money flowing and remain operationally sound in a downturn.

After all, it is a lot easier to strategically reduce costs than it is to shift from losing money in good times to being profitable in bad times.

Companies that normally lose money face existential going concern risks during an economic downturn. And even those that are normally profitable can still face risks to their profitability — and their existence.

But their chance of survival is greater.

The trick is to keep the money flowing.

Cash flow is life.

After all, the only way a business fails is if a company runs out of money and it cannot pay its bills or service its debts.

SPEND ANALYSIS

CHAPTER 4

GETTING NUMBERS TOGETHER

The first step of any analysis project is asking the right questions and collecting the right data.

When trying to cut costs, you begin with spend analysis.

And in a spend analysis project, there is one central data question: Where do I find the excess spend that I can cut to boost profitability?

This isn't just relying on financial statements.

It is about going one or two or three levels deeper. It also means that you might need to go beyond what auditors would even do in terms of testing and sampling.

After all, sometimes auditors miss stuff. Testing and sampling are often not as complete and comprehensive as the spend analysis consultants will do.

After all, consultants doing a cost leadership project don't have to decide if company statements fairly present the value of the company.

But they do need to find areas of excess spend. That is the core question: Where do I find the excess spend that I can cut to boost profitability?

But that isn't the actual starting point for data analysis.

The actual question that needs to be asked before collecting data for a spend analysis project is: Where do I find the most complete collection of accounting, purchase order, and expense data available for my company?

This is the core question, because you need to get very granular data to find the opportunities.

As some consultants I know like to say, "There are riches in the niches!"

Collecting Data

Only after asking the more specific question above about comprehensive accounting, purchase order, and expense data can you really move on to beginning to collect the data.

As you begin the next step to collect data, you need to think about where your data is coming from. When you are using internal data, you need to make sure that the data is appropriate.

If the company data you find doesn't answer the question, then you will need to keep on digging. But there can be many different issues that crop up during the data collection process.

You may also find inconsistency of data records, data units, data systems, and data collection.

In terms of systems, some companies may keep their records in a sophisticated accounting software program like SAP, while others may keep their records in Excel sheets, or they may be paper copies.

Worse still is if a company has its financial and accounting records in different systems. And there can also be incomplete data records. Although this can happen if a business has moved or been involved in a natural disaster, it is more common if the company uses systems people don't know how to use properly.

This can occur because the system is too complicated — or new.

Additionally, you may find that the data you are working with is comprised of incomparable data sets, which could lead to an apples-to-oranges comparison — and provide misleading implications.

You need to be very careful about this kind of data problem. After all, if the data sets don't match up and you do analyses, the implications could be misleading, outright wrong, and straight-up worthless.

Interviews

One of the most important parts of any spend analysis project is often interviews of key personnel. This may include the executive team, the finance team, procurement, human resources, and other leaders.

Often these interviews provide you with information on where to find data for your analysis — and they provide you with context and content that you might otherwise miss.

There's a saying among consultants that somewhere in a company, someone knows the answer to the problem you are trying to solve. In this case, someone or someones within the company likely know exactly where costs can be cut — and why.

This means that any consulting project — as an internal or external consultant — is a bit like a hunt for clues. In essence, you talk to a few people, and they refer you to other people, who refer you to still other people.

By the end of this sleuthing process, you will have found key people who can provide you with actionable recommendations. And finding those key people can go a long way to helping collect qualitative information to support the purely quantitative operational and accounting data you collect.

On more than one occasion, I've sat down with executives who directly told me about spend levels that were too high and needed to be examined.

Executives have also often pointed out where data might be inconsistent as well. Plus, sometimes leaders in operations can even physically point you directly to assets that are ripe for repurposing, redeployment, or disposition.

In truth, leadership often has an inkling as to where excess spend or waste may be, but they don't want to be the ones to make the call on their own. They want to have their assumptions tested and proven right — or wrong.

In any case, they sometimes want a neutral third party to make the recommendations about cutting costs. This is why external consultants are often brought in. But even internal analysts or consultants may be tasked with finding the areas of excess spend.

It serves much the same purpose, but it can be a bit trickier politically for the employees performing the analysis and making the recommendations.

Next Steps

After you have pulled together all the data you need from the financial systems and the people within the company you are analyzing, it's time for the next step: checking that the data you are working with is appropriate, reliable, and trustworthy. After all, this is a necessary precondition in the next step of data analysis: cleaning your data.

CHAPTER 5

CLEANING THE DATA

The most important thing about doing a deep dive into financial records is to make sure you are doing it right. This is why the first step for any kind of cost-cutting, as well as the associated spend analysis or data analysis, is to make sure that the data you plan to use is also "clean."

In other words, you need to be sure that the right data has been collected, that the data has been properly organized, and that it is consistently and accurately recorded.

Data that isn't clean can taint the results of any analysis you might wish to conduct.

This is why cleaning data is a critical part of any data analysis process that you don't want to skip.

This means that your data needs to be consistent, use the same units of measure, be for the same time period, and be formatted correctly.

Questions to Consider

Some questions you might ask as you perform due diligence on your input data might include the following:

- Are the columns and rows of data all in alignment?
- Does the data show the right units of measure?
- Is everything in the right currency?

If there are inconsistencies in your data, you may need to make adjustments to the data, eliminate some data from your analysis, or select new data you could use or create to perform the analysis required.

Cleaning your data is critical because it will help to make sure you don't run into any issues when conducting the analysis.

It also improves the usefulness of any analytical implications, and it can prevent your need to redo analysis from scratch if data problems are discovered later.

It can cause a huge headache if someone skips ahead to analysis without cleaning the data to be compatible with the technical tools being used.

Misaligned columns can yield faulty results when run through a statistical software package.

Especially in a world of cloud computing, where you may be paying for the ability to complete an expensive or high-value analysis, you don't want to waste your time and on-site or remote processing power by putting data that isn't clean through the process.

That's a waste!

But there is a much bigger reason to make sure your data is clean.

The Logic Behind Clean Data

Have you ever heard the phrase "Garbage in, garbage out"?

This is what happens if your data isn't clean.

Your results might be garbage.

That's why only after your data is clean can you move on to actually analyzing the data.

And if your data is not clean, then you may need to recollect the data. After all, you want to make sure that your analysis yields something fruitful, which is highly unlikely if the data is all messed up.

Such data that isn't clean is also referred to as "dirty" data.

And you don't want the presence of dirty data to force you to have to start your project all over again from the beginning.

Or worse.

You do not want to derive false implications of the spend data that could lead to management decisions that have potentially deleterious impacts on your company.

Specialized Questions for Spend Analysis

Aside from the broader data questions to address when preparing data for spend analysis, there are also specialized questions that need to be answered, including the following:

- Is there some spend data that isn't categorized?
- Can the uncategorized spend data be categorized?
- Are all the purchase orders properly categorized?

When doing this kind of analysis, it is important to make sure that you put data in the right buckets.

When thinking about making the right decisions for cutting costs, you will need to have targets and goals, comparable figures, and the right baseline to start from.

But you can't compare spend data that isn't properly collected or in the wrong bucket.

For example, you might identify areas of above-target spending that may have been miscategorized. In such a case, you could be cutting something essential.

Breaking Down Costs

Spending usually focuses on total costs, which for assets is often abbreviated as TCO, which stands for the total cost of ownership.

But for the kind of analysis required to identify potential cost-savings opportunities, it is best to break down costs into as many subcategories as possible.

Labor Costs

For labor costs, you need to make sure that all labor costs are properly categorized, breaking out the following costs:

— **Salaries for employees**
— **Straight-time full-time wages for employees**
— **Overtime full-time wages for employees**
— **Part-time wages for employees**
— **Overtime wages for part-time employees**
— **Full-time wages for contractors**
— **Part-time wages for contractors**
— **Overtime for contractors**
— **Payroll taxes**
— **Healthcare benefits**
— **Retirement benefits**
— **Fringe benefits**
— **Other labor costs**

One area of labor costs not included here is executive compensation. That is very often an off-limits topic, as you might imagine. I discuss other off-limits topics in Chapter 8.

Equipment Costs

Beyond labor cost considerations, it's important to break down equipment costs in the smallest categories possible.

This includes a breakdown of as many elements of TCO as possible, including:

— **Purchase costs:** What you pay for the equipment you own.
— **Finance costs:** What you pay in interest to finance the cost of the equipment you own.
— **Rental costs:** What you pay to rent equipment.
— **Service costs:** What you pay as part of a service agreement for the equipment you own or rent.
— **Maintenance costs:** What you pay to maintain the equipment you own or rent.
— **Parts costs:** What you pay for spare parts for equipment you own or rent.
— **Staffing costs:** What you pay for specialized staffing for the equipment you own or rent.
— **Fuel costs:** What you pay in fuel costs for equipment you own or rent.
— **Storage costs:** What you pay in storage costs for equipment you own or rent.
— **Insurance costs:** What you pay in insurance costs for equipment you own or rent.
— **Training costs:** What you pay to train your people to use equipment you own or rent.
— **PPE costs:** What you pay in PPE costs for equipment you own or rent.
— **Other associated costs:** What you pay in all other costs for equipment you own or rent.

Software Costs

In addition to labor costs and equipment costs, software costs should also be analyzed and categorized. These include:

— License costs

— Special hardware costs

— Training costs

Implications

Breaking down expenses and putting spend in the right categories are critical to ensuring the highest probability of successfully identifying cost-cutting opportunities. Furthermore, dirty data of all sorts, including incomplete, incorrect, and miscategorized data could inform inappropriate, costly corporate decisions, investments, or strategies.

CHAPTER 6

PRIORITIZING SPEND CATEGORIES

Once you've cleaned your expense data, you will need to put the expenses into consistent buckets. After that is done, you will need to prioritize your spend categories.

In short, you need to identify which buckets of expenses are part of the core business — and which categories of spend are nonessential.

Sometimes it's tough to tell where the opportunities are, but there are a few things that analysts and consultants look for.

Primarily, when I've done projects like this, I'm looking for outlier expenses. The questions I ask to uncover the greatest opportunities include:

— Is there a category at the top of the spending list that is not critical for the company?

— What do "the usual suspects" for cost-saving opportunities look like?

— Are there expenses in a category that seem excessive or frivolous?

Nonessential Spending

The first place to look at spend is in nonessential spending. If your top areas of spend are not related to your core business, then you want to earmark those categories for deeper analysis.

This means if you're in manufacturing, but your human resources or marketing spend is greater than your cost of goods sold, you may wish to consider a deeper evaluation of what is essential for your business.

In a service business, some overhead expenses — like fancy offices or company cars — may be completely unnecessary. Of course, for some businesses, these may be essential requirements. And they may be material to keeping current clients happy. But this is where a deeper evaluation of expenses is required.

The Usual Suspects

Beyond the top areas of spend analysis that may or may not be essential, in almost any spend analysis, there are a few critical categories that should be evaluated and examined for cost-cutting opportunities.

The round-up of the usual suspects for cost-cutting includes:

MRO

This stands for maintenance, repair, and operations. It includes preventative, corrective, and predictive maintenance as well as all the associated and relevant parts. It is most important for manufacturing, industrial, and light industrial companies.

There are all kinds of expenses in MRO, and it is one of the spend categories that companies struggle with the most. Sometimes these expenses are run up in a desire to never stock-out of parts.

After all, needing parts you don't have is a pain. And rather than take risks of downtime, companies often overstock.

Other times, MRO expenses can rise due to a lack of judicious use.

Finally, MRO expenses can sometimes also be elevated because parts are "growing feet," as they say.

Unfortunately, this is also a not uncommon occurrence with personal protection equipment — otherwise known as PPE — like gloves, goggles, and hard hats.

Equipment

It is very common for companies to own more equipment than they need. It is also common for there to be excessive spare parts, forgotten service agreements, mothballed equipment, and other problems.

Companies tend to take a buy-it-if-you-need-it approach when business is good. No one wants to hold up equipment purchases — even if they are excessive — when revenue may depend on having that equipment.

Holding up the process may just not be worth the effort. But in a downturn, it's time to take a look at what's on the balance sheet, in the office, in the field, in the shop, and in the yards.

Overtime

When considering labor, looking at overtime as well as maintenance hours and contractor expenses are top priorities for opportunity.

Essentially, these are all procyclical labor expenses.

It is not uncommon for companies to let overtime hours run excessively high in good times, before needing to clamp down on excessive overtime hours when the economy slows and supporting profitability falls on the shoulders of strategically reducing spend.

Similarly, contractor expenses and maintenance hours tend to be procyclical. And when the economy is strong and business is good, their spend is greater.

But the value of these expenses should be evaluated if there is less revenue, less business, and generally less work that needs to be done — all of which is common in a slowdown.

This topic is of greater focus in Chapter 19.

Contracts

Another area to potentially address excess spend is in contracts.

Most companies have difficulty naming their top vendors, let alone describing when they last reviewed or renegotiated their top contracts. This is the focus of Chapter 10.

When business is slow, it's time to revisit contract terms and potentially renegotiate with vendors.

Travel and Entertainment (T&E)

This is usually one of the juiciest categories for cost-cutting opportunities. When the economy is good, sales guys and gals are usually set loose to run wild. A good economy is usually positively correlated with increased revenues.

And that's when authorizing extra meals, nicer client events, high-end parties, and endless drinks makes the most sense from an ROI standpoint.

And while fancy dinners at New York's Keene's Chophouse or renting out the Tao nightclub in Vegas seem reasonable when everyone is living high on the hog, they seem beyond excessive when the economy slows and revenues are unlikely to be impacted by whether an open bar is serving Johnnie Walker Blue — or Johnnie Walker Red.

It might even be time to switch over to beer — or iced tea.

Extreme Examples

Of course, there may be much more extreme examples of travel and entertainment expenses in your company's budget.

There may be a very high-end client retreat or incentive trip for your best salespeople to somewhere exotic that was planned when the times were great.

But if layoffs are a risk, those trips will seem frivolous. And they are likely be canceled.

Of course, I've seen big changes in the approach to T&E over the years.

For example, shortly after I started working in investment banking in 2004, I received an email instructing everyone that strip club expenses would no longer be reimbursed.

I was shocked that they ever had been.

And not long before that, it was still legal in some European countries to deduct the cost of foreign bribes from corporate taxes. In France, bribing foreign officials was legal until September 2000. In Germany, it was legal until December 1997.[1]

The point here should be that there should not be any T&A on your T&E report.

And this isn't just true for the guys.

Female colleagues shouldn't be expensing those tickets to the *Thunder from Down Under* show in Vegas.

The thunder needs to be at the bottom line of your business.

At some points in the business cycle, all of the entertainment expenses in the world won't generate new business.

Significant Value

In most of the spend analysis projects I've conducted, most of the main areas to reduce cost are in the priority areas I've outlined in this chapter.

That's not to say that there isn't more — or even a lot more.

But when you look at your company's expenses, or those of a company you are doing consulting work for, you need to be sure to examine MRO, equipment, contracts, overtime, and T&E. Because there is sure to be value — and likely significant value — to uncover in those areas.

CHAPTER 7

BENCHMARKING COSTS

In addition to looking for excess spend and cost-savings opportunities in a number of proven categories, another great way to uncover value is by benchmarking the costs in different spend companies for your company against the costs in certain categories across your entire industry.

There are a few different ways that cost benchmarking occurs. But it almost always involves the collection, analysis, due diligence, and reporting of anonymized data by trusted sources, including industry groups and consulting firms.

My company, Prestige Economics, has done this kind of cost and risk benchmarking for industry groups on behalf of their members.

But I've also seen other consulting firms do this kind of cost benchmarking directly for a cohort of companies.

The goal isn't to get the biggest number of participants.

The goal is to get the greatest number of similar participants that will all provide accurate data.

If the data isn't accurate, the benchmarking will be skewed, and decisions made on that information will not be the best.

Furthermore, if the benchmarking data collected is not anonymous, such a project could be viewed as non-competitive, and it may even violate antitrust laws.

Cost Leadership is the Goal

The priority for companies participating in the benchmarking of costs isn't just to know what the spend of other companies is.

It's also important to see the comparative levels of spend — as well as a range of spend within that industry. Only by seeing the industry standard and that range can a company engaging in a cost leadership project begin to aim for benchmark averages or the lower end of the benchmarking range.

This kind of comparative analysis in industry standards can be made for any number of categories, including overall operating expenses, capital expenses, fixed costs, marginal costs, labor costs (including overtime), MRO, and T&E.

If a company providing a higher-quality product than the average company in the space can achieve costs at or below the benchmarking level, this could result in significant increases in profits — and it could even lead to an increase in market share.

Low-Cost Supplier Versus Cost Leader

A low-cost supplier is competing purely on cost in an industry. But that isn't the only way to be evaluated as a vendor. And that isn't the goal of cost leadership.

The goal of cost leadership is to have some of the lowest costs in an industry. And it's also to try and achieve those lower costs while delivering above-average value.

As with other parts of a spend analysis project, the road to achieving value from a benchmarking project and benchmarking costs begins with questions and data.

CHAPTER 8

OFF-LIMITS TOPICS

In every company, there are topics that are off-limits when doing a spend analysis project. You might be looking for ways to cut costs and help your company become a cost leader. And you may find some big ones.

But there are always sacred cows. There are always off-limits topics.

If the areas for strategic cost-cutting are off-limits, keep looking for opportunities.

Sensitive Topics

Some of the most common sensitive topics include:

— Executive Compensation
— Shareholder Dividends
— Raw Inputs
— Layoffs
— Special Projects
— Critical or Regulated Expenses
— Other Categories

Executive Compensation

This is one of the most common off-limits topics when doing a spend analysis or cost leadership project. It's common because the odds are good that executives are the ones driving the project.

Executives may be your main stakeholders as a consultant. Or it may be your own leaders, who have asked you to find areas to cut costs.

Shareholder Dividends

Shareholders own the company. And they may be very dissatisfied if their dividends are cut. This is especially critical in publicly traded companies.

Not only is the goal of public company executives to act in the best interests of shareholders, but executive compensation is likely to be tied to equity market performance.

Even in private companies, it is highly unlikely that the owners or shareholders would be willing to fully forego any profits or dividends — as they may need them to live off of.

Raw Inputs

This is commonly off-limits for companies that turn a raw material into a finished product.

This would be a reason refinery spend analysis would exclude crude oil prices. After all, turning oil into product is the business.

This is also the reason a power company's spend analysis might exclude the cost of coal or natural gas.

After all, the refinery and the power company are price takers in those markets, and buying the raw materials is critical to their core businesses.

Similar exclusions may also be seen in companies that buy industrial commodities on the open market, including metals like scrap metal, iron ore, copper, or aluminum.

Companies that buy agricultural goods may also exclude the cost of foodstuffs traded on commodity markets, like cocoa, coffee, corn, sugar, soybeans, and more.

Layoffs

This topic is usually off-limits — but it might not be for the reason you expect.

In fact, there are four big reasons why layoffs might be off-limits.

First, layoffs might be off-limits because the company does not want to implement layoffs. The owners or executive leadership might want to leave the workforce fully intact.

Second, layoffs might be an off-limits topic because the company has planned layoffs and does not want to discuss or disclose this to the team of internal leaders — or external consultants — doing the spend analysis and cost-cutting project.

Third, layoffs might be off-limits because the company does not want this to be considered because the potential for layoffs has not yet been decided.

Finally, layoffs may be off-limits because company leaders do not want workers in the company to be concerned about how a cost leadership project could impact their jobs, and subsequently withhold data from the team doing research and making recommendations.

Special Projects

Sometimes special projects are considered off-limits. This might include a major technology implementation that cannot be easily stopped — like an SAP conversion that impacts financial record-keeping and accounting data.

Of course, it might also be a construction project, like building a new warehouse or factory. Or it could be a multiyear robot, automation, or AI implementation project.

Critical or Regulated Expenses

In addition to the other off-limits categories, there are some areas where cutting costs is much more difficult. These include areas that are critical for legal, accounting, and compliance reasons.

In general, these areas of spend are not optional. And while the potential to change vendors for services may be an option in some cases, it may very well not be in others. Legal, payroll, audit, and many other vendor changes will be unlikely.

In truth, most companies choose to leave these areas outside of potential cost-cutting consideration.

Other Categories

In addition to all of the off-limits spend areas discussed in this chapter, there is a significant potential for the company's leaders to exclude other categories from analysis.

My advice is to leave off-limits topics alone and just accept the exclusions set by the stakeholders of the cost leadership project. Instead, just focus on the areas where cost-cutting is allowed.

Because that's all you can do.

So, just make cuts where you can!

Your Own Decisions

In addition to excluding spend categories at the direction of the client, you may also be tasked with identifying areas of spend analysis that are out of bounds.

There can be any number of reasons for this, including the reasons previously listed in this chapter. It may be as simple as the fact that your client has not circumscribed areas for analysis and exclusion.

I've avoided jargon in much of this section of the book, but I now need to introduce the more formal terms for areas of spend that are included in your analysis as well as those that are excluded and otherwise off-limits.

Addressable and Unaddressable Spend

Areas of spend that are considered inbounds for analysis purposes are the focus on the project you will be running. The term for this kind of spend is **addressable spend**. This is because you will be addressing these categories during your analysis.

The areas of spend that are excluded or off-limits in your analysis are considered **unaddressable spend**.

In Figure 8-1, you can see how I have often shared this concept with clients. The hypothetical unaddressable spend shown represents 43 percent of company spend, while 57 percent is categorized as addressable.

The addressable spend is then broken down into big buckets of spend categories.

Of course, this is just one of the charts we use when doing spend analysis and cost-cutting or cost leadership projects. We also paid this with a further breakdown of categories in the addressable categories. And we use financial waterfalls, with the unaddressable categories highlighted.

The point of these kinds of breakdowns is to highlight what we can attack — and to leave the rest aside, exactly as I noted above.

Seeing color-coded breakdowns is very helpful for clients to recognize and identify opportunities to reduce spend. And that leads to a greater probability of leadership buy-in and action, which is critical for a cost-cutting program to be effective.

Figure 8-1: Addressable and Unaddressable Spend

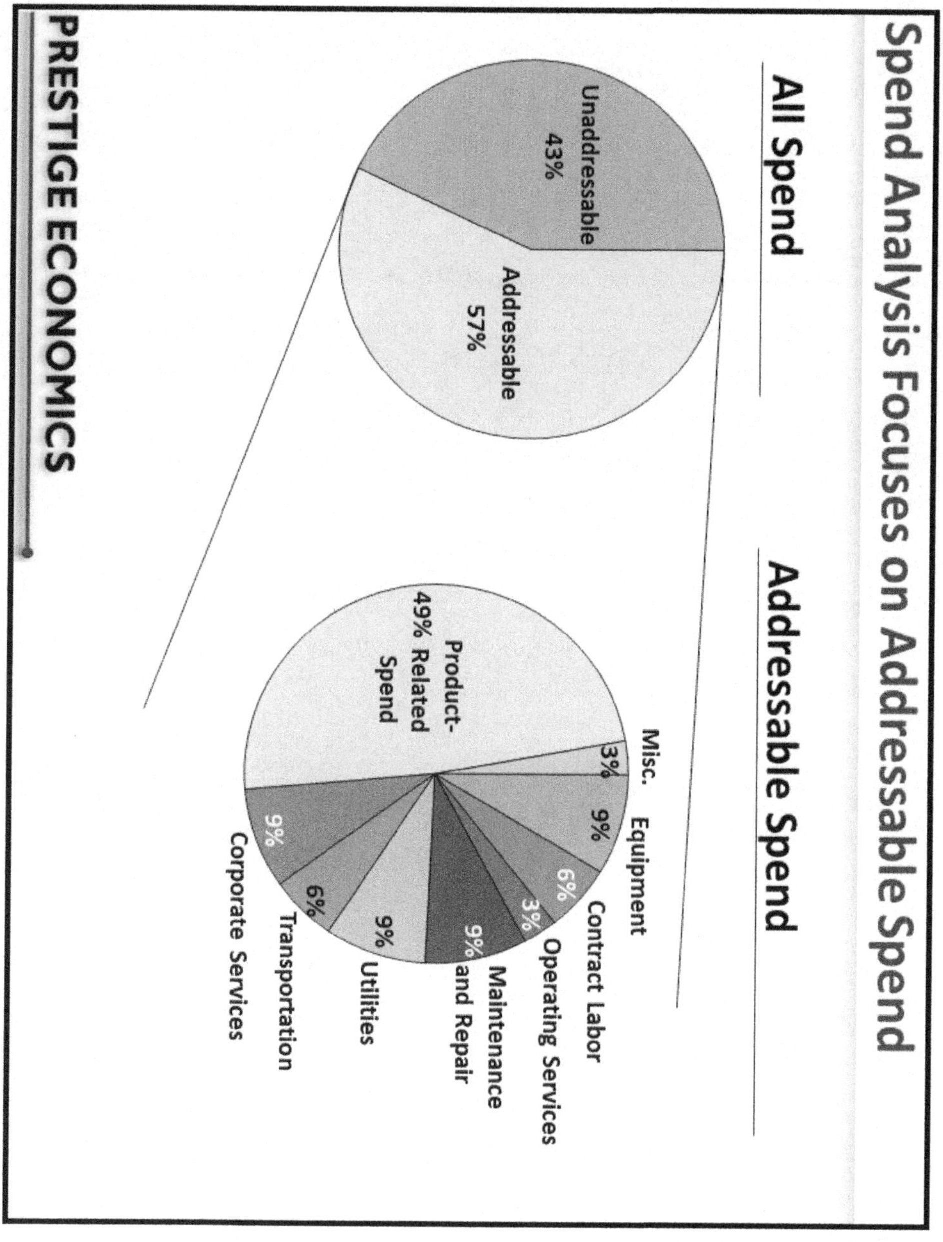

CHAPTER 9

STRUCTURED PHASES

In this section of the book, I've tried to focus on concepts and process, rather than laying out too much jargon — or too much formal structure. But it is important to talk about how you might want to structure a spend analysis project for your company — or as a consultant to another organization.

In Figure 9-1, you can see a four-phase project that I have laid out. This isn't the only way to do a spend analysis. But it is a way that has worked for me on a number of different occasions.

The four phases my team and I use when doing a spend analysis project could best be described as follows:
— **Phase 1: Data Collection**
— **Phase 2: Data Cleaning and Categorization**
— **Phase 3: Data Analysis**
— **Phase 4: Presentation of Results**

Again, you can set your own framework for this. There isn't a hard and fast set of rules on this. But the process should roughly mirror the chapters in this section of the book.

After all, before you can present results (Phase 4), you need to actually perform your analysis (Phase 3). And before you can analyze data, you need to categorize and clean your data (Phase 2). And none of that can happen without collecting the data and ensuring you have a complete picture of the data, including financial records and interviews (Phase 1).

There is one other thing that you need to also include as part of your data collection process, and that's visiting the physical facilities of the client if possible. It's the same thing you would need to do if you were performing due diligence or audit.

You just need to be there.

In visits to physical facilities, I have often discovered inefficiencies of operations, assets that could be subject to recovery and disposition, as well as other opportunities related to excess spend, like overstaffing.

Consultants doing this work bring fresh eyes to the problem and may be more likely to see opportunities that internal employees or executives may have not noticed or considered. But if you aren't working with a consulting firm and you are doing your own analysis, you should visit all of your physical operations. And you should try and do it with fresh eyes. Asking lots of questions helps identify opportunities.

And the most valuable question in a spend analysis is "Why?" Keep asking like a child until there is no answer. When you get to the end of the question line, you'll probably have hit pay dirt!

Figure 9-1: Four Phases of a Spend Analysis Project

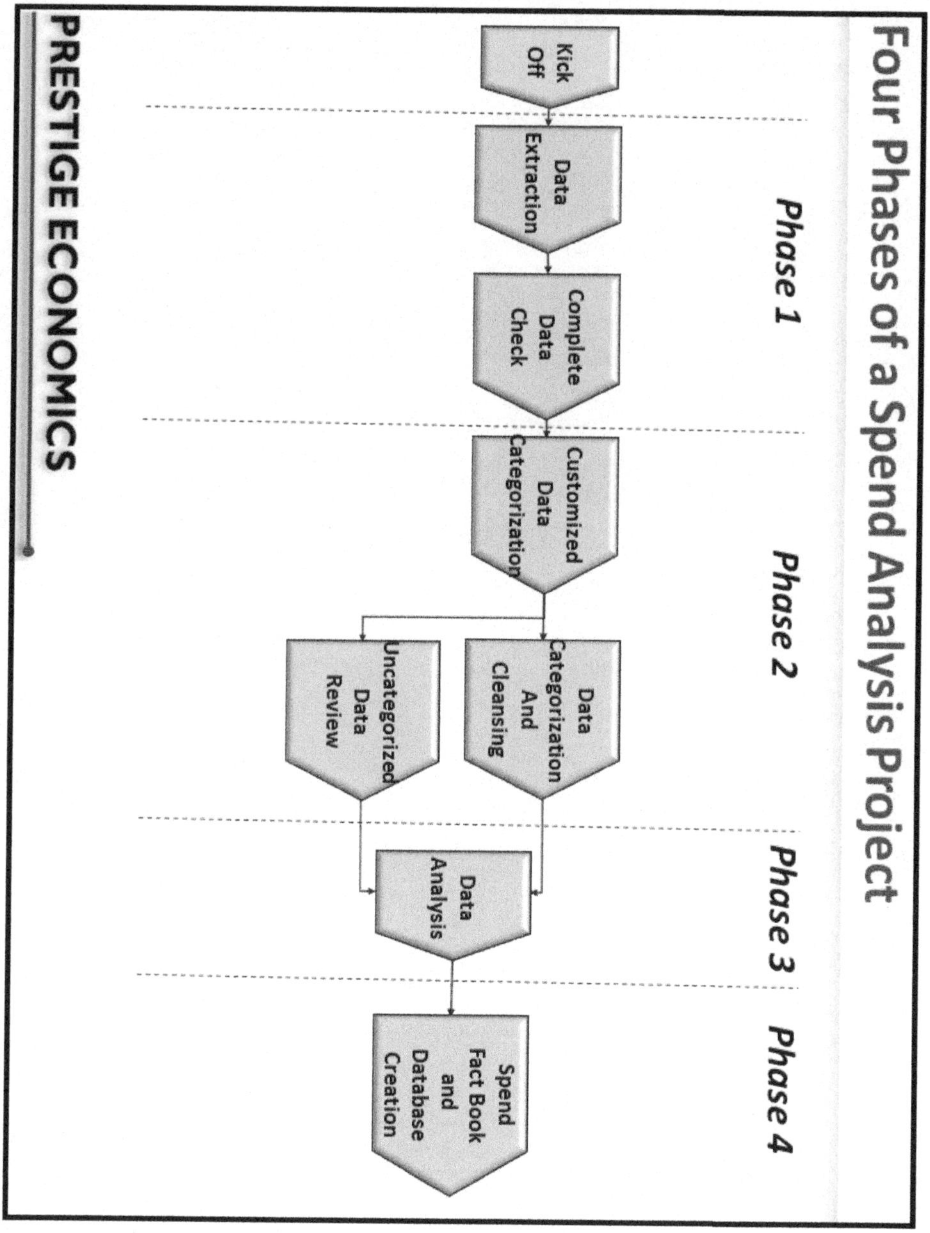

MAKING CUTS

CHAPTER 10

PRIORITIZING VENDORS

Before cutting costs, it's important to prioritize your vendors.

This isn't just a consideration of cost either. And there are several ways to prioritize and rank vendors.

Cost should be a consideration. But so should quality and reliability. In short, you are looking for vendor value — not just the lowest-cost vendors.

In truth, this is the other side of the cost leadership coin that was discussed in Chapter 7. You are looking to identify the best performer relative to the price point. Creating vendor scorecards is an effective way to get there.

Vendor Scorecards

One way to evaluate vendors and rank them is to have the purchasing department, executive team, or company owner fill out scorecards that rank vendors in a number of ways.

Scorecard Criteria

Some of the criteria often included on a vendor scorecard include the following:

— **Vendor Importance**
— **Vendor Reliability**
— **Vendor Consistency**
— **Vendor Speed**
— **Vendor Payment Terms**
— **Vendor Cost**

Defining these terms will be important for making the most effective scorecard.

Not all of these criteria need to be weighed equally on the scorecard. And additional priorities for vendor evaluation can be uncovered in a discussion with procurement or purchasing. Some of these may be irrelevant, and some of them may be much more critical. Or they may all be equally important. Let the client help set those terms.

Vendor Importance

One of the top criteria when evaluating vendors is how important they are. If you can live without them, that's very different than if you can't.

This is one of the stickiest considerations, and it is the reason why many companies do not use sole sourcing. In the process of doing a spend analysis project, it is important to consider if there are other vendors you are not using.

Procurement leaders often refer to the strategy of vetting potential vendors as "three bids and a buy." In short, it means that at least three vendors should be considered for each major purchase.

And this is doubly true for ongoing purchases.

Being too reliant on any one vendor presents various kinds of risks, like supply chain risk. And it reduces your ability to negotiate terms.

Vendor Reliability

The reliability of a vendor is very important as well. A vendor you can count on as highly reliable is much more valuable.

Vendor Consistency

Knowing that a vendor provides a consistent product or service is critical for any business operation. An inconsistent vendor adds cost to business operations, either in terms of wasted time or replacement costs.

Vendor Payment Terms

Some vendors are paid 30 days net. Others are willing to except more favorable purchasing terms, like 45 days net, 60 days net, or 90 days net.

Vendor Cost

This is what most people consider first when evaluating vendors. And it is important. But it is not the only factor to consider, as you have hopefully seen in this chapter.

One critical goal of building a vendor scorecard is to establish values for various vendors so you can build a negotiation plan.

An example of a scorecard can be seen in Figure 10-1.

It includes both the categories articulated in this chapter as well as a weighting metric that can be applied to the subcategories to separate the prioritization of importance from the performance of the vendor. The card uses a simple five-point scale for the weighting and a 10-point scale for performance.

The total value for a vendor is essentially the sum product of these values.

Implications

Once you have determined the values of the vendors, you can develop a strategy for the negotiation process. The rankings are important because you may be more willing to negotiate firmly with lower-scoring vendors while treading more carefully with higher-scoring ones.

And negotiation strategies are the subject of the next chapter.

Figure 10-1: Sample Vendor Score Card

Vendor Scorecard

VENDOR NAME

VENDOR ATTRIBUTES	Weight 1 to 5		Performance 1 to 10		Points
Importance	#	X	#	=	#
Reliability	#	X	#	=	#
Consistency	#	X	#	=	#
Speed	#	X	#	=	#
Payment Terms	#	X	#	=	#
Cost	#	X	#	=	#
Total Points					

PRESTIGE ECONOMICS

CHAPTER 11

NEGOTIATING WITH VENDORS

In most negotiations, the party that cares the least has the most leverage.

And so it is with cost-cutting.

This is why creating vendor scorecards is valuable. Because you gain better visibility into where you may have leverage — and where you may not.

Among negotiation experts and academics, there is a term for this: BATNA. It stands for the best alternative to a negotiated agreement. It is of prime importance when considering any kind of negotiation.

Basically, it means that you need to know what your best alternative is if you cannot come to an agreement. And if you have alternatives that are pretty good, you can be a tough negotiator. But if your next-best option is poor, then you need to be more careful in your negotiation strategy.

Of course, there are ways to improve your BATNA, like finding new vendors or substitute products or reducing your demand for a good or service.

Assistance at Arm's Length

One of the main goals of a spend analysis project is to use data to sever relationships. It is designed to keep vendors and customers at arm's length.

Essentially, spend analysis is designed to help you break relationships that result in contracts not based on pure, raw, tough financials.

Sometimes companies bring in firms like mine to find inefficiencies and control for them.

This often involves several parts, including:

— **Monitoring Costs**
— **Analyzing Costs**
— **Negotiating with Vendors**
— **Pushing Back on Vendors**

Have you ever had a conversation with someone, and they aren't your client but they push back hard on their behalf?

The company managing costs is supposed to do the same thing: push back, push back, push back. Often. They get a cut of the money saved, so they want to push back as hard as they can.

A very aggressive example of this is signing up for a gym membership — and then trying to cancel it.

If you've tried to cancel a gym membership, then you probably know what I mean. When you sign up, everything is great. The people are nice. The contract is easy.

But canceling a gym membership is almost always handled by an outside vendor. One that is explicitly tasked with contract enforcement.

When I moved to Germany in 2007, I tried to cancel my gym membership in Charlotte, North Carolina.

I was required to provide proof that I had moved. And one of the potential items I could provide would be a utility bill. So, I mailed in a utility bill from my new German address.

Since I was living in Germany, the bill was in German. And the company tasked with preventing my cancellation claimed since it wasn't in English, it was not proof that I lived somewhere else.

Implications

As you can tell from my story above, being a tough negotiator can be effective. But there can often be a cost. It can strain vendor relationships. But sometimes it's just not worth it — especially if you are very reliant on that vendor for your business or if that vendor performs particularly well on your scorecard.

CHAPTER 12

REVERSE AUCTIONS

In addition to using data for negotiation purposes, it's also possible to use technology in the negotiation process to apply pressure on vendors. One common way to do this is to have vendors compete against one another in what's called a reverse auction.

These aren't like typical auctions for cattle or fancy works of art, where a fast-talking auctioneer gets people to bid against one another, offering higher and higher prices until the highest price wins.

Reverse auctions go quite the other way.

Sellers bid for the prices at which they are willing to sell their goods or services. And at the end of the auction, the seller with the lowest amount wins.

Reverse auctions also go by another name, Dutch auctions, because these auctions originated in the Netherlands.

Reverse auctions reduce the prices companies pay for goods and services. But it is also important to make sure that the quality of the goods and services is up to par.

After all, you might want a cost leader that provides the relatively highest-value goods and services, and not just one that's the lowest-cost provider.

One way to ensure that a reverse auction goes well is to have specific vendors apply in advance. Then, you allow your preferred, qualified vendors to bid. This helps ensure the expected quality of the goods and services you will receive.

Often this is done by using software to set up the reverse auction online and setting an appointed time for the auction to occur.

Doing this in real time provides an immediate call to action for potential vendors, especially because they can see the prices changing.

In real time, this is usually shown as a price increasing. And the first vendor to bid on the rising price wins the contract. This provides a lot of pressure for vendors, because if they bid too early, they might not make a profit because the price is too low. But if they bid too late, they might not make a profit because they don't get the contract.

This puts the buyer — your company or client — in a much more favorable position to keep costs competitive.

Sealed Bid Auctions

Beyond the use of reverse auctions, there are also sealed bid auctions. But these are likely to be less effective than online reverse auctions for achieving the best prices possible.

For sealed bid auctions, anonymous bids are submitted by a deadline. Of course, there are no price changes to see, which is why this presents less pressure on vendors than showing them price changes in real time online.

This is why reverse auctions usually result in better outcomes.

Implications

Whether you employ sealed bid auctions or reverse auctions, either choice is likely to result in more competitive pricing than just accepting vendor prices without question — or negotiation.

CHAPTER 13

EXITING CONTRACTS

One last ditch resort to consider in the face of costs that you cannot afford is the potential to exit contracts.

I'm not talking about breaking a contract or violating an agreement. I am specifically referring to exiting a contract.

This is following the terms of an agreement to buy your way out of it. Exiting a contract usually has costs. But the cost to end an agreement may be worth it. The costs may be much less, in fact, than the cost to continue to follow the terms of an agreement with a vendor.

If your agreements — or your vendor agreements — do not have buyout or cancellation clauses, I strongly suggest you add them.

Additionally, you should add mediation and arbitration clauses to all of your agreements. In case there is a dispute or disagreement, it's important that everyone know the costs, the terms, and the steps that follow.

Even if an agreement does not have a buyout clause, you can always go to your vendor and ask to exit an agreement. Often, there are terms that will satisfy both parties. And sometimes, finding out what those terms are is just a matter of asking the question.

Working with Your Vendors

In addition to asking your vendors about exiting agreements, it is also possible to ask vendors to revisit the terms of the agreements you have in place.

I'm not talking about strong-arming or making a fuss.

I'm just saying: You can ask.

By asking nicely, you may find that long-time vendors are willing to amend or change their terms due to exceptional economic circumstances.

The outcome of such a discussion could hinge very much on which party is larger — and how important the business is.

If you represent the bigger party to the agreement, a change to your contract could materially hurt the smaller party during a recession. This could give your vendor little wiggle room, and it could, in fact, give your vendor little choice but to enforce the terms of the agreement.

Such a situation could impact your vendor to the point that they go out of business.

If they are a critical vendor for your operations, forcing them out of business would be a heavy price to pay to reduce some of your costs.

However, if the other party to your agreement is much bigger than you are, they may have more flexibility to accommodate your situation — especially if their flexibility could keep you in business.

Implications

Due to recent slowing business activity, various companies and organizations will try to exit their contracts. But many of them may not have legal grounds to exit them. After all, pandemics are often an exception to force majeure clauses in many agreements.

Your organization may want to exit its own contracts, but there are only two different honorable ways to approach contracts that you can no longer afford to fulfill: You can buy your way out or ask your way out.

Either way, a contract is a contract. And if you're unhappy with the outcome now, all you can do is strive to write better contracts in the future.

Some contract terms you may wish to consider in the future are take or pay agreements or contracts that offer options with financial benefits for both parties, like power interruptability contracts.

CHAPTER 14

REDUCING PHYSICAL OVERHEAD

One critical way to reduce company costs is to reduce unnecessary overhead. This includes reducing office space, inventory space, warehouse space, retail space, and any other square footage that is not absolutely necessary for your business.

I've kept the overhead of my business, Prestige Economics, extremely lean since I founded the company 11 years ago.

In fact, for the first four years of the business, I operated out of an 800-square-foot apartment. My computer desk was part of the same granite countertop as the cooktop directly adjacent to my workspace.

In the last two locations since leaving that apartment, I have continued to maintain a home office — but no additional, separate commercial office space.

We have never had an office. And there have never been any plans to get one.

It just hasn't been necessary for my business, even if some of my former colleagues thought it was strange to found a business without an office in 2009.

I thought it was the most normal thing in the world to do.

After all, people have been able to work remotely for some time. And when I started worked in consulting at McKinsey in 2007 — almost 13 years ago — many consulting firms, including my own, were letting people work from home, and they were already using flex space and coworking spaces.

But many corporations have resisted the move to remote working environments.

With recent developments, this decision makes me feel a great deal of affinity for the motto "I'd rather be lucky than good."

We are now at a watershed moment. And while the ability to have large remote working staff has been a potential for many years, companies that resisted the move are now being forced to adapt.

Going forward, many companies will likely be unable to wind the clock backward.

Of course, some companies will never look back.

From a cost leadership standpoint, why would they want to?

Many companies are likely to support remote working long into the future because it reduces corporate overhead and increases worker satisfaction and flexibility.

Benefits of Reducing Corporate Overhead

There are a number of major cost savings associated with increasing the number of remote workers and reducing the size of physical operations.

The benefits of remote work include reducing direct real estate costs as well as:

— Reducing water use and costs.
— Reducing paper products use and costs.
— Reducing power consumption and costs.
— Reducing internet costs.
— Reducing food and meal costs.
— Reducing parking needs and costs.
— Reducing the need for an office gym, company coffee shop with barista, game room, etc.

In short, some business basics as well as some of the greatest perks seen in startup life culture could become antiquated trappings of a far-too-luxe period of time.

In addition to lowering costs, these use reductions can also help companies meet increased pressures for ESG and sustainability goals.

Plus, remote workers may be able to afford a significantly higher quality of life without needing to live close to an office in an expensive area.

If you never have to go to an office in Manhattan or Silicon Valley, you can get a high wage and still live far out in the country.

The only thing that matters is your access to the internet, a computer, and a phone.

For companies, this also presents a financial advantage. After all, if you make Manhattan profits but can pay your people wages that are competitive for Boise or Milwaukee, you may be able to reduce your labor costs significantly while keeping your profits high.

Other Cost Implications

While reducing physical overhead in terms of office space is critical for businesses like mine, the importance of reducing square footage needs for any kind of company can also deliver significant financial value.

In the wake of recent disruptions, retail space demand could also fall — even if warehouse and distribution center square footage demand is poised to rise.

The truth is that the highest-cost square footage, especially in heavily dense urban areas, could experience a decline in demand.

Beyond Square Footage

One way that I've repeatedly highlighted some companies gain leverage in their day-to-day operations is to use technology to control other costs wherever possible.

One important example of this is the use of vending machines for PPE cost-savings programs. Not only does this reduce some MRO square footage, but it also helps track the use of MRO and PPE equipment. These are goods that are notoriously difficult to track — and they often grow legs.

Being judicious in overhead can greatly improve company profitability. After all, every dollar in spending that gets cut goes right to the bottom line. This means that cutting costs can actually boost profit more than increasing sales.

ASSET RECOVERY AND DISPOSITION

CHAPTER 15

ASSET RECOVERY

There's a phrase that applies to asset recovery; "Waste not, want not."

As opposed to the other ways of improving company profitability, asset recovery doesn't involve negotiating with vendors, cutting spend, or cutting people.

Asset recovery involves a three-step process to recover the value of assets that are not being used to their greatest potential.

This process includes:
— **Asset Identification**
— **Asset Redeployment and Repurpose**
— **Asset Disposition and Divestiture**

In short, this is the corporate equivalent of reduce, reuse, and recycle. It is a hunt for hidden value in assets a company owns and may not be fully optimizing. Asset recovery is a process, but it can reveal tremendous value.

CHAPTER 16

ASSET IDENTIFICATION

Asset identification is the first part of asset recovery.

After all, before you can improve the value of an asset, you need to identify assets that are not being used to their fullest potential.

There are many kinds of assets that can be repurposed, redeployed, or divested.

And they fall into six general categories.

These include:
— **Heavy Equipment**
— **Office Equipment**
— **Software**
— **Inventories**
— **Physical Plant**
— **Other Assets**

Let's take a deeper look at each of these categories.

Heavy Equipment
Some of the highest-value assets that can be identified for asset redeployment, repurposing, and divestiture are capital equipment.

This category of goods includes construction equipment, heavy machinery, trucks, cars, forklifts, backhoes, shredders, oil and gas drilling equipment, and any other heavy assets.

There are many different levels of waste that come up in asset identification.

And some of these levels are absolutely ridiculous.

First, some of the goods may not be in use. This would make it possible to repurpose the goods so they could be used. The best strategy here would be to use them or sell them.

Second, some goods might be needed, but they do not work. These could be repaired or sold. Or if they are in really bad shape, they could potentially just be recycled.

Third, some goods might not be in use and not working — but they may be *rented*. In this case, the company is paying for a rental agreement on broken equipment.

That's a big waste!

Reviewing the rental agreement is critical. And exiting the rental contract may likely make the most sense.

Fourth, some goods might be not in use, not working, rented, and with a maintenance or service agreement.

That's an even bigger waste.

The rental, maintenance, and service agreements should all be reviewed — and potentially exited in part or in total.

Fifth, some goods may be not in use, not working, owned, and with a maintenance or service agreement.

As in the case of rentals, the maintenance and service agreements for this owned equipment should be reviewed and very potentially exited.

Sixth, some goods may be not in use, not working, owned with a maintenance or service agreement, and paying for insurance on them.

These costs should all be reevaluated, and agreements should be reviewed and potentially exited. Once excess equipment is disposed of, insurance agreement terms should be renegotiated.

Office Equipment

Beyond heavy equipment like construction equipment, machinery, and vehicles, there are also various kinds of office equipment that may be identified for potential repurpose, redeployment, or divestiture.

As opposed to vehicles and heavy equipment, this could include lighter, high-tech equipment like computers, copy machines, automated vehicles, robots, or other equipment.

These assets can also be repurposed, reused, or divested.

Software

Beyond hardware, there are also software licenses and subscriptions. Although it seems unlikely that software could be divested, they could be repurposed or redeployed.

Inventories

As with physical assets, excess inventory, inventory that is no longer useful, and inventory that no longer has value can all be considered for redeployment, repurposing, or divestiture.

Of course, some assets will be easier to sell, like commodities. But the value of other assets could still be monetized.

Physical Plant

These are some of the most valuable assets that a company could sell. These could include office buildings, manufacturing facilities, retail buildings, and any other kind of physical building or facility.

Especially if a lot more people begin working remotely on a permanent basis, we could easily see companies look to dispose of office buildings and other forms of commercial real estate.

Other Assets

There is no limit to the types of assets that can be repurposed, redeployed, or divested. Any asset a company is not using to its full value is a potential option.

As you can see, there are many different kinds of assets that a company may be able to identify for repurposing, redeployment, or divestiture.

And a big part of maximizing the profitability of a company is to make sure that you are getting the greatest value possible out of all the assets on your company's balance sheet — especially the highest-value assets.

And that's what happens next — after you've identified the assets that could produce greater value.

CHAPTER 17

ASSET REDPLOYMENT AND REPURPOSING

The goal of asset redeployment and repurposing is to find ways to put underutilized assets to work.

Maybe there are some vehicles not in use at one physical site that are sorely needed at another site. Redeploying them could increase the value of underutilized balance sheet assets.

And the more valuable an asset is that gets redeployed or repurposed, the more value that is likely to be created for the company when it gets redeployed.

I have seen numerous clients shift around assets between facilities to optimize operations. This is often done in concert with other strategic cost-cutting.

By shuttering one facility and consolidating assets at a more productive facility, there can be heavy costs. But there can also be an increase in profitability, due to an increased concentration of the highest-value assets.

Another example of repurposing assets is increasing the utilization of more efficient assets and reducing the use or utilization rate of less productive assets.

This can be true in a manufacturing facility, where a more productive line is run more, and a less productive line is run less.

And it can also be true in a scrap yard, where more efficient bailers or shredders are prioritized over less efficient ones.

Using Assets on Hand

Beyond consolidating the highest-value assets, or increasing the utilization of the most productive assets, sometimes asset redeployment is just deploying assets that are on hand — but not currently in use.

I have sometimes seen companies purchase cost-saving equipment that had never ever been deployed in the first place. And by deploying — by using — that equipment, the company was able to generate income statement and cash flow benefits that had previously been overlooked.

The money was already spent, but no one took a close look at all the equipment and assets at the facilities.

Internal managers missed it. External auditors missed it.

But there was this equipment just sitting in a corner.

Unused.

And it had never been used — not once.

The reason?

Simple enough: After the equipment was purchased, no one completed the required training to operate it.

This may sound unbelievable, but think of all the times you bought a piece of workout equipment you didn't use. And then there are apps and computer accessories you might have sitting in a box somewhere.

Well, sometimes it's the same thing with companies.

They have assets they aren't using; despite the potential value they could bring.

That's what repurposing and redeploying assets is all about.

CHAPTER 18

ASSET DISPOSITION AND DIVESTITURE

Asset disposition and divestiture is the process of getting rid of assets by disposing of them or selling them.

In truth, there are many reasons to get rid of assets. Let's look at a few key reasons you might want to get rid of an asset and earmark it for disposition or divestiture:

— **Unprofitable**: It is an unprofitable asset or part of your business.
— **Low ROI:** The asset or part of your business has a lower rate of return or lower ROI than other parts of your business.
— **Expensive:** It is an unnecessary asset or part of your business.
— **Risky:** It is too risky an asset or part of your business.
— **Distraction:** The asset or part of your business detracts from your core competencies.
— **Unnecessary:** It is an unnecessary asset or part of your business.
— **Useless:** It is a useless asset or part of your business.
— **Unenjoyable:** You don't like the asset or part of your business.

As you can see, there are any number of reasons to get rid of an asset. Some of these are primarily financial considerations, like if the asset is unprofitable, has a low ROI, or is expensive.

But there are also operational reasons to get rid of an asset, like if it is risky, a distraction, unnecessary, or useless.

And, of course, you may just not like the asset — and you want to get rid of it.

The truth is that you may find any number of reasons satisfactory enough to get rid of an asset. But in a downturn, the most important motivation is usually to free up cash flow, reduce balance sheet liabilities, and increase profitability.

Let's look at some examples for each of these cases.

Unprofitable Assets

This is pretty straightforward. If you have an asset or part of your business that is losing money, you may want to sell it — or just dump it. While this is true at any time, you can't afford to have assets that lose you money in a downturn. After all, that's when you need cash the most.

If you opened a subsidiary of your business in good economic times and it's been consistently losing money hand over fist ever since, a downturn may be exactly the time to give up the ghost. If it couldn't make hay while the sun shined, try to sell the business. But even if you just close the doors and shut it down, that might be worth it as well.

The goal of strategic cost-cutting in a downturn is simple: Just don't run out of cash.

And an unprofitable asset is operating antithetically to that mantra.

When thinking about divesting an asset or part of your business that isn't profitable, be prepared to accept the fact that you might not be able to get much money for it. After all, if it's losing money for you, it might lose money for someone else as well.

So, if you can't find a buyer, don't worry about it. Just stop the financial bleeding and move on.

Even just one finger in the dike holds back some water.

Low ROI Assets

Assets with low ROIs are not as bad as assets that are not profitable. After all, an asset with a low ROI is still making money. That's a lot better than an asset that is bleeding the cash you need to hold out for the next upturn in the economy.

But a low ROI asset is one that isn't the most efficient deployment of your capital. Honestly, you always want to put your best dollars to work. But this is especially true during a downturn, when credit usually gets tighter, and money needs to be put to its best use possible.

Don't tie up too much money in an asset with a lower rate of return than you could get elsewhere.

On the upside, an asset or part of your business with a low ROI is still profitable. So, you don't have as urgent a need to address the problems with this asset or part of your business as you do with unprofitable assets.

It is still making money after all.

The good news about getting rid of a low ROI asset, however, is that if it's profitable for you, it is likely to be profitable for someone else as well. And while you may think the ROI is low, someone else may be very happy with the potential rate of return. This gives you a higher chance of selling a low ROI asset.

This can have one big benefit if you sell the asset: You may be able to recover cash from the asset and deploy it elsewhere in your business to generate a higher rate of return than you are currently getting.

Of course, if the ROI of the asset is relatively low but you wouldn't be able to get a better rate of return elsewhere in your business or investments, then you may want to just accept the low ROI and hold on to the low ROI business. In that case, holding on to the asset is your least-worst-case scenario.

Expensive

Even if an asset has a high rate of return, it may be too expensive to maintain during an economic downturn. This is especially true if the asset requires a rental fee or financing payments that exceed the revenues you can achieve in a downturn.

Again, this all comes back to making sure you are deploying your capital effectively and efficiently. And a big piece of capital equipment that brings in a strong rate of return may still be too expensive to maintain.

Or it may be too expensive to justify to shareholders.

An example of this might be a private jet. After all, a private jet can save you a lot of time, and if enough people are traveling on it, it can be cheaper than flying commercial. But during a recession, the optics of private jets for public company shareholders are not great.

I recall during the Great Recession when automakers went to Washington, D.C., to ask for bailout money. Some of them flew in on private jets. And that did not go over well at all. Showing up hat in hand is one thing. Showing up top hat in hand is another.

There is one big problem with divesting an expensive asset during a downturn: You aren't likely to get anywhere near the full value you would be able to capture during good economic times.

But depending on the asset, you may not have much of a choice.

Risky Assets

Some assets present big financial or operational risks. Think of equipment subject to frequent breakdowns, equipment subject to malfunctions, or equipment that requires very high insurance premiums. An example here to consider might be a roller coaster.

If you own an amusement park, the carousel is a probably not your riskiest asset. But some monster roller coaster that goes upside down a few times very well could be.

And while you may be willing to tolerate the riskiness of the asset when the economy is good, if attendance at your theme park is low because of a weak economy or social distancing, you might decide that the juice is not worth the squeeze for your roller coaster.

After all, your insurance premiums are likely to be very high. And if you have lots of people coming to the park to ride the roller coaster, it might be worth paying those premiums — and taking the risk of running the coaster.

But if you are running it virtually empty and no one is coming to your theme park anyway, you may want to mothball the asset and shut it down. Or you may want to sell it to another theme park that is more than happy to pay handsomely for it.

There are many examples we could give like this in the industrial world, like tractors, forklifts, or shredders that are just sitting around idle because of a slowdown. They are still risks to have around — and because they are relatively dangerous (compared to say office equipment like computers and monitors), the insurance premiums on them are likely to be high.

For these reasons alone, it might be worth putting them into secure storage, selling them, or even just recycling them.

Distraction Asset

Have you ever heard of the 80/20 rule? This applies to a few different things in business.

On the one hand, people like to say that 80 percent of your business comes from 20 percent of your clients.

But they also say that 80 percent of your problems comes from 20 percent of your business.

Fortunately, the 80 percent that brings the revenue is often not the same 80 percent that brings the problems. In fact, I've often found it to be quite the opposite, insomuch as the 20 percent of the problems often come from the least important parts of your business's revenue.

When this happens with an asset, it's something I consider a distraction asset.

That small-dollar subsidiary that eats up all your time. That one piece of equipment that isn't very useful — but somehow sucks up a big chunk of your MRO budget.

This kind of asset can be an ROI problem, or it might just be a big distraction because of lawsuits, labor disputes, environmental issues, or any other of a host of problems that can require lots of attention, distracting you from the goal of maintaining profitability across your business.

Or it may be as simple as an asset that is taking too long to figure out.

Remember, your only goal is to remain flush with cash and focus on profitability and cash flow.

Everything else is a distraction — especially a distraction asset, which some might refer to as the "problem child" of your business.

The good news is that you may be able to sell distraction assets to someone for whom the distraction is a core competency. But even if you can't, if the asset is hurting your ability to focus on returns elsewhere in your company — or if it is consuming too much of your time — you may need to divest yourself of the asset or otherwise shut it down.

Unnecessary Assets

Another reason people often divest or dispose of assets is that they simply aren't necessary. Maybe they were at one point in time, but they aren't anymore.

Movie theaters used to use analog film projectors, but now they largely use digital projectors. Sure, you could keep the analog projectors for the rare instance when you are showing a movie on actual film, but chances are you don't need to hold on to all of your old film projectors.

And this isn't to say that these assets are useless. They aren't. But having a lot of them is quite unnecessary, given the current state of technology.

We could probably say the same thing about office fax machines.

You just don't need as many as you used to.

For unnecessary assets, the values in disposition or divestiture can vary greatly. In the above examples, you are dealing with older technology, and the recovery value is likely to be quite low.

But other unnecessary assets might be oil and well drilling equipment in a mature oil field. If all the wells are drilled, you don't need new drilling equipment. And while that equipment may be unnecessary for you, if it's in good condition, it might be quite valuable for someone else.

Useless Assets

Maybe you have an asset that adds no value to your business. You bought it for a line in a factory that no longer exists. Or you bought specialized equipment for someone who no longer works at your company.

There are two kinds of useless assets: Assets that are useless for you and assets that are useless for everybody.

First, let's consider assets that are useless for you.

For example, maybe I bought a farm that came with logging equipment and chain saws. But I have no idea how to engage in logging. Furthermore, I have no interest in logging; I just want to raise cattle. For me, the logging equipment would be useless.

But for a company or individual focused on the logging business, acquiring these assets could bring real value.

There are many kinds of assets that can be useless for you.

For example, a piece of equipment that requires another piece of equipment to be functional. In this case, it could be put into use, but on its own, it is deficient. This is like buying a silverware set that somehow includes all of the spoons and knives but none of the forks.

In a disposition of this asset, it may have value above and beyond scrapping it. But it may not.

And there are broken pieces of equipment as well. Some of these assets are useless to almost anyone.

Over the years, I have visited a great number of industrial, light industrial, warehousing, and manufacturing facilities. Most of these facilities have broken-down equipment.

And I've seen this a lot!

Sometimes the equipment is beyond repair, sometimes spare parts can no longer be acquired for the equipment, and sometimes the equipment still has a service contract tied to it, even though the service company doesn't have any skilled mechanics for the broken-down equipment.

In each of these cases, it may be best to consider recycling, disposal, or disposition of useless asset. But you should not expect to turn a pretty penny on useless assets that are — for all intents and purposes — useless for everyone.

Unenjoyable Assets

This may sound like the most frivolous reason that a company might divest itself of an asset. But it's not. I'm sure you've donated things or sold things on eBay that you just didn't enjoy. This is pretty much the same thing — but at the corporate level.

These kinds of assets might be considered nuisance assets rather than the aforementioned category of distraction assets. Maybe part of your business is split between the two coasts, and you are sick of traveling. Or maybe you are getting ready for retirement, and you don't want to manage certain assets anymore. In that case, you may just decide to sell the asset. It isn't enjoyable and you want out.

To provide a tangible example, my pool guy recently sold part of his business in South Austin. When I asked him why, he told me, "The money was good, but the traffic was horrible." It wasn't about the money; it just wasn't enjoyable. Anyone who owns a business feels like that about some of their business at least some of the time. And when the hassle becomes too great, they sell.

The good news is that if you're selling a profitable asset that is a fundamentally sound business, you can probably get a decent price if you can be patient.

Takeaways

There are a lot of different reasons to divest assets. And when you do, it frees up value tied up in assets, putting more cash on your balance sheet. Plus, it can also free up business cash flow — and deploy capital more efficiently, to boost profitability.

LABOR COST-CUTTING

CHAPTER 19

LABOR CONSIDERATIONS

Flexibility in business operations and spending is the name of the game when it comes to outlasting a recession. And having flexibility over labor spending is critical because it is typically one of the biggest areas of addressable spend for most companies.

None of these options are pleasant, but it may be worthwhile considering them. At the most basic level, a company can cut worker wages, hours, or both. There is also the potential for a company to cut cash bonuses, retirement benefits, and other costs related to labor. There is an extensive discussion of a relatively easier cut, reducing overtime, in Chapter 20, whereas the much more difficult task of implementing layoffs, is the focus of Chapter 21.

In order to properly address labor cost optionalities and opportunities, it is critical to break down labor costs, including salaries and wages, healthcare and retirement benefits, bonuses, payroll taxes, fringe benefits, and all other costs.

Performance-Based Incentives

In addition to cutting overtime, straight-time hours, or wages, it is also possible to tie income more directly to company revenue and profitability with performance-based equity incentives.

As previously discussed, during a downturn cash is king. So, even if you are going to tie compensation to profitability, you may wish to offer equity incentives rather than cash incentives. This has four key benefits.

First, equity compensation reduces risks to your cash flow. After all, companies don't go out of business by offering up too much equity. They only go out of business by running out of money and being unable to pay their bills. By offering equity over cash, you are inherently reducing cash flow and income statement risks that can present a greater opportunity for a company to weather a recession or economic slowdown in the near term.

Second, recipients of equity will also align their personal incentives with a company's survival into an expansionary period, because equity payouts only happen if the company survives and grows.

Third, some equity incentives have a vesting schedule or performance-tied thresholds. This means that equity in the company may not immediately be granted to the recipient. Plus, the equity may not be granted to the employee or executive if they are not at the company long enough to see the equity incentives vest — or if the incentives turn out to have no value.

Fourth, performance-based incentives reduce the chance of free-riding staff. If workers only get the benefits if they perform, then there is a higher chance that they will strive to meet those goals.

The use of performance-based incentives and equity is one of the main ways to compensate executives. But during a downturn, it may be worth considering this kind of compensation for the broader staff of your organization.

The Worker Perspective

It is important to consider the impact of labor cost-cutting from the worker side as well. After all, in a downturn, workers who are not laid off may end up working more hours than before the recession. And if they are salaried, this means that their effective hourly rate would fall.

Early in my career, I had a job that paid about $150,000 per year. It was a good job with good income. And at 40 hours per week, or 2,000 hours per year, it would have been about $75 per hour, which is very good indeed!

But I wasn't working 40 hours per week. I was working 100 hours per week. And at 100 hours per week, or 5,000 hours per year, the hourly wage would have been only $30 per hour.

I might have been able to earn that much waiting tables.

But it was worse for others. For example, I had friends during the last recession working 80 hours per week without doing actual paid work for clients — and without hope of promotions.

In any case, sometimes keeping workers on the payroll but giving them excessive amounts of work to do can also cut their effective hourly rate.

But it can also make workers head for the doors — especially if they don't see any long-term opportunities. Again, this might be a reason to offer performance-based equity incentives in tough times.

Remote Work

One of the final labor considerations I have discussed at length in this book is the potential to have people work remotely. While this can help you significantly reduce your overhead, remote work also makes it easier to let go of people you don't have to confront face to face.

But that opportunity can be a double-edged sword. After all, if you don't treat them well, remote work can also make it easier for your people to walk as soon as the economy recovers too.

CHAPTER 20

REDUCING OVERTIME

One of the areas I mentioned earlier as a prime category of excess spend is overtime.

This is what I consider to be one of "the usual suspects" because it's not uncommon for companies going through an expansion or growth spurt to give it the gas, as they say. The push is on growth, and costs are secondary compared to a potential capture of additional revenues.

Plus, during an economic expansion, it can be difficult to find additional staffing resources. The job market is hot, and new people are tough to find — or too expensive to justify hiring.

For these reasons, among others, companies boost overtime as a way to tap into additional flexible capacity at a time when capacity is tough to come by.

But when the going gets tough, and revenues fall, it's time to start analyzing labor market spend data — especially overtime.

After all, it is a lot easier to hire people in a recession. And employers may have access to a better pool of candidates at more favorable wages. So, if the company does indeed need the man hours, there would probably be a bigger financial benefit to reducing expensive overtime hours and just hiring additional staff that may be highly qualified at a much lower price point.

This dynamic of running up overtime in good years but the need to pull it back during a downturn is particularly important for industrial, light industrial, supply chain, and manufacturing businesses, where many of the staff may be hourly as opposed to salaried.

But this is a dynamic that can be seen across industries.

Theme parks, retail stores, hotels, casinos, and many other procyclical businesses may be willing to pay a premium for man hours when the money is flowing in. But when the economy slows and cash flow is tight, overtime should be cut.

This is also an important prophylactic move that can preserve the jobs of the workers on staff. After all, before you consider layoffs, you could at least pull labor costs down from straight time plus overtime to just straight time.

This can also reduce benefits costs as well, if there are employee retirement programs that have contribution matches determined by percent of income. If overtime is cut, income is cut. And if income is cut, the maximum retirement contribution — and employer match cost — is cut.

Just because cutting overtime hours may sound like an easy cost to cut, it may be quite painful for some of the workers who rely on the overtime income to pay their mortgage, auto loans, or other bills.

But it is better than layoffs.

Some companies I've done spend analysis projects for discovered massive levels of overtime hours and intentional, systemic overtime hour allocations to help workers hit a certain total compensation level.

If that is a goal the company wants to meet, so be it. But that will need to be considered.

More often than not, companies may not be paying a lot of attention to overtime hours — especially when revenues are up, and the economy is expanding.

For example, when I worked at Walt Disney World way back in the mid-1990s during the earliest parts of my career, I was able to work the overtime system to gross more than $1,000 per week. And that was with an hourly wage of only $5.65 per hour.

It wasn't easy. But it happened.

There were all kinds of extra levels of overtime that could be earned during holiday weeks. But there were all kinds of special names for the hours I worked, like double time, triple time, holiday double time, holiday triple time.

It was ridiculous.

And that is exactly the kind of craziness you need to be on the lookout for when you are analyzing the overtime spend.

Keep in Mind

The most important thing to keep in mind is that cuts in overtime will adversely impact your people. But if your company doesn't make it, no one will have a job — overtime, straight time, or any time.

CHAPTER 21

LAYOFFS: THE LAST MOVE?

Layoffs are horrible.

You stop paying staff, they file for and collect unemployment, and then they try and find a new job.

And layoffs are doubly horrible for workers during an economic downturn.

After all, the time those former workers might be on the unemployment rolls before they're able to get a job interview — let along get a new job — is likely to be significantly longer than during an economic expansion.

And while layoffs are horrible for the workers who lose their jobs, layoffs aren't just bad for the workers who get laid off.

They are also bad for the workers who remain. And they can be bad for the long-term prospects of a business as well.

Layoffs and Workers That Remain

You might be thinking that it's callous to say that layoffs are tough on the workers who don't get laid off.

But it's true.

And there are three big reasons for this.

First, the workers who remain behind often live in fear that they could be laid off next. This adds a lot of pressure to their working lives.

Second, workers who don't get laid off are often expected to pick up the slack. The euphemism for this is to "do more with less." So, in addition to being stressed out about being potentially laid off in the future, the workers who remain behind are also often pushed to do a greater volume of work.

This isn't a great situation either, but workers are likely to find themselves stuck between a rock and a hard place.

Third, if you are going to get laid off in a downturn, the truth is that it's better if it happens earlier in the recession. After all, the later into a recession you get laid off, the more unemployed people there will be.

That means there will be increased competition for jobs that are likely to offer lower compensation. And you will very likely need to wait longer to find a new job than if you had been laid off earlier.

The irony is that if you get laid off first — just as a recession is starting — you probably are going to have a greater chance of finding a new job than people who get laid off in the second, third, or fourth round of layoffs.

Employer Impacts of Layoffs

From an employer perspective, layoffs are extremely negative as well. And they are usually a last resort to keep a company alive. All of the other ways to cut expenses, get cash on the balance sheet, bolster cash flow, and improve profitability should be taken before implementing layoffs.

After all, in addition to the stress of laying people off, employers know that they are adding stress to their workers — and potentially creating conditions that undercut future employee loyalty. Plus, they are losing valuable talent that could contribute to high demand or growth when business opportunities reemerge.

Any employer worth their salt knows that their most valuable resource is their people. And that good people are immensely difficult to find. The loss of valued personnel, coupled with increased uncertainty and the prospects of employee distrust of their employer, can sow seeds that limit growth opportunities in a future economic recovery and expansion.

So, layoffs really are bad for everyone: those who are laid off, those who remain, and the employers who have to see the layoffs through.

FORWARD-LOOKING STRATRGIES

CHAPTER 22

TWO PIECES OF ADVICE

I wrote this chapter to share two critical pieces of advice with you that matter more during a recession than at any other time during the business cycle. First is some business advice.

One Piece of Business Advice

The advice I have to share is simple enough: **Just don't run out of money!**

I know that I've articulated this advice at other points in this book. But I just can't stress it enough. The truth is that companies that can survive recession often come out much stronger on the other end.

Being able to function in a lean economic environment casts a long shadow on the growth, development, and expansion of a business.

I know that it greatly impacted how I built Prestige Economics — and how it still runs today.

But it's more than that.

In truth, some of the biggest and most successful companies in the world were founded during recession. Sometimes this may have been sheer happenstance, but often new businesses are formed during recessions because of lowered opportunity costs to engaging in new ventures.

Of course, while some of the most successful companies were founded during recessions, many companies also died during recessions.

And the goal is to make sure your company doesn't die.

You need to make sure that you hold on.

Because if you can make it through a downturn, the growth, the business, the revenues, and the profits will very likely be much higher during the next uptick in growth.

Look, most businesses don't do well in recessions. But most people didn't go into business to make their money during recessions. That would actually be a pretty horrible strategy in general, because recessions don't happen most of the time.

In fact, recessions are relatively rare and short compared to periods of economic growth and expansion. And that's a good thing, because businesses usually only need to hold on for a little while before having a much longer period of sustained growth.

There is, of course, one other reason not to run out of money for your business: It would lead to your unemployment, and the bankruptcy of the business could negatively impact your future professional job options. For example, if you're a C-suite executive, your career might go down with the ship, even if only the company dies metaphorically.

One Piece of Jobs Advice

This consideration is tied to my second piece of advice, which is for workers, employees, and even executives.

It's also quite simple: **Just don't get fired!**

Layoffs are tough on everyone, but they are most difficult for people who lose their jobs. And there's even something worse than just losing your job.

It's called unemployment scarring.

In short, when you become unemployed, the future trajectory of wages you might have had will be negatively impacted. And your future trajectory of wages will shift lower. Plus, the longer you remain unemployed, the more negative and more long-lived the impact will be on your future earnings.

So, even though getting laid off early in a recession is better than getting laid off later in that same recession, the best situation for your long-term income and career prospects is to not get laid off at all. Hence my easier-said-than-done recommendation: Just don't get fired!

CHAPTER 23

CUTS TO AVOID

As you consider potential costs to cut, it's important to make sure that you don't cut anything essential that could hurt your company during a recovery phase.

For each business, there will be some cuts that are essential to avoid. And many of these may be the out-of-scope, unaddressable spend in a spend analysis and cost-cutting project.

Or it might be that the assets tied to these activities are also sacred cows that cannot be put on the asset recovery and disposition block no matter what.

But aside from critical company-specific assets, people, physical plant, and other spend that is deemed essential, there are also a number of other categories of expenses that you should not cut — no matter what.

Audit, Accounting, and Finance Expenses

At the top of this list are audit expenses, accounting expenses, and software that makes the accounting, bookkeeping, audit, and financial operations of your company functional.

Your business could do essentially nothing. It may sell all its physical plant, trademarks, and patents. And it may fire all its people — including many of its finance people.

But as long as there is money in the bank and a way to keep track of financial records, and there are controls and processes in place to remain legally and financially compliant with state and federal laws, you probably won't go to jail — even if your business fails.

If you lose the ability to track funds, you lack financial controls, your money vanishes, or you do something illegal with those funds, you could be in real trouble.

Even more important than having a profitable business is making sure that you don't go to jail.

In fact, this is the very first level of the CEO hierarchy of needs in Figure 23-1. It's even more important than the next two levels up, which were the focus of the previous chapter.

Security Costs

Other areas that you probably shouldn't cut are security costs. This is for much the same reason as keeping complete and accurate financial records. You need to secure your physical plant. and you should protect the assets you have.

Last Resorts

Beyond financial and security expenses, it's also important to try and keep from cutting any core workers until the very end. After all, without them, it might be impossible to restart your business.

Similarly, you don't want to cut anything — like paying interest on outstanding debts — that could hurt your business or personal credit scores. Having bad credit can greatly hinder your ability to operate a going concern. And this is to be avoided.

After all, if you lose your core workers and you have bad business credit, you may not really have a business anymore. And at that point you should consider permanently closing your business.

Figure 23-1: CEO Hierarchy of Needs

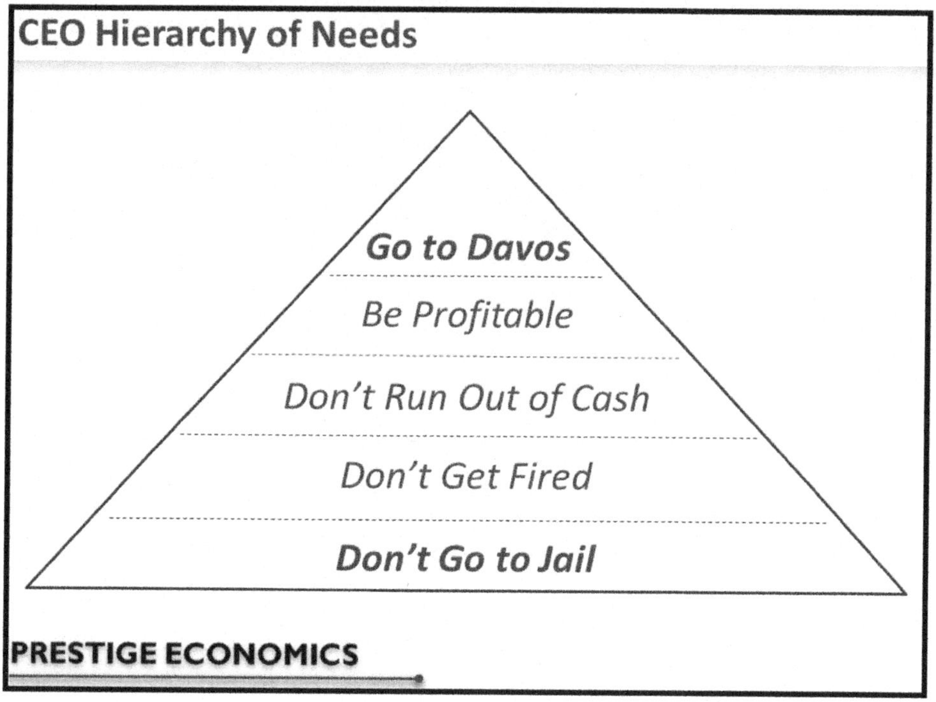

CHAPTER 24

LIMIT THE DOWNSIDE

Economies expand far more often than they contract, so planning for the upside is one of the most important things you can do — both in good times and bad. And during a downturn, this means limiting the downside risks.

Economic Resilience and Cyclicality

The name of the game in surviving economic downturns is being resilient and being flexible.

It's about staying in the game long enough to see the benefits of economic recovery and expansion. One critical step to fostering resilience in a downturn is to understand what kind of business you have and how your business performs at different parts of the business cycle.

Additionally, it's important to understand what kinds of clients are likely to perform the best in good times, bad times, or regardless of the timing of the business and economic cycle.

There are three distinct kinds of businesses that are typified by their relationships to growth and profitability during the business cycle. These include:

— **Procyclical Businesses**
— **Countercyclical Businesses**
— **Acyclical Businesses**

Procyclical Businesses

These businesses tend to move in favor of the economy. And these are the vast majority of businesses. Your company — or your corporate clients, if you are a consultant — are most likely to be procyclical businesses.

The good news about procyclical businesses is that they do very well during the longer expansionary phases of the economy. But they perform poorly in downturns.

If you have a procyclical business, you might want to try and serve clients in countercyclical or acyclical businesses as a hedge against recessionary declines in overall economic activity — and a potential drop in your overall business performance.

Countercyclical Businesses

Countercyclical businesses tend to perform counter to the economic cycle.

This means that they do their best in a downturn, but they experience a marked slowing during economic expansions.

There are very few truly countercyclical businesses. But thrift stores, junk food, and liquor stores to do better in downturns. Education is another countercyclical business.

After all, many people who lose jobs in a downturn may seek to upskill and get more education to improve their future professional lot in life after the economy recovers.

Of course, the biggest countercyclical client you can have is the government. After all, the government usually uses fiscal stimulus to support economic growth during an economic downturn. And governments often engage in the highest levels of spending — deficit spending, in fact — to boost economic growth.

Governments often take on debt to deploy funds to support GDP growth in a recession. But the source of the funding is not nearly as important as the fact that governments increase their spending at a time when other businesses are unable to spend.

Having government clients can be strategically wise during an economic downturn. Although government contracts can be complicated and payments may be slow coming, compared to some corporate clients, the funding agreed to is much more certain than funding promised by private or public companies.

Acyclical Businesses

If you don't have the ability to serve countercyclical clients or do countercyclical business, you might be able to service clients that have acyclical businesses.

Acyclical businesses tend to have performance that is relatively uncorrelated with the business cycle.

Some important acyclical businesses include food, utilities, and healthcare. These are some of the most basic consumables in society; they are the most fundamental ingredients of economic growth.

Additionally, software businesses — especially those with software as a service (SAAS) business models — are also usually acyclical. The goal with SAAS models is that the ongoing cost should be low enough to prevent a discontinuation of a service.

Pulling It All Together

While your business is likely to be procyclical and your clients may be generally procyclical as well, the best way to protect against — and limit — the downside is to acquire clients that are in countercyclical or acyclical businesses. Of course, you can also push your own company into acyclical or countercyclical lines of business or industries. That should help you hang on long enough for the next recovery and expansion to begin.

CONCLUSION

STRATEGIC COST-CUTTING

The big idea in writing this book was to share actionable strategies to help you improve the profitability of your company — or your client — by strategically approaching the problem of costs and profitability during an economic downturn.

Hopefully, the analytical frameworks and actionable strategies and tactics I have laid out in this book will help you get there.

And I hope this book helps your business.

A recession is very likely upon us now. And this one may be somewhat different than other recessions in recent history, as this recession was induced more or less by government decree for the benefit of the public good and public health.

But however different this downturn or recession may be, it will still be likely marked by an overall decline in business activity, a rise in joblessness and the unemployment rate, and a drop in consumer spending that may last months or quarters.

Of course, the current situation is rapidly evolving, and the path forward and the government response as well as the impact on business and the economy are uncertain.

One thing seems certain, however: Many industries, businesses, individuals, and economies will be seriously impacted in the near term. And the near-term costs will be high. Yet, however long or short the latest economic and business downturn lasts, it will most certainly not be the last downturn. After all, economic activity occurs in cycles.

Plus, the economy and financial markets tend to exhibit a dynamic that finance professionals and traders refer to as "escalator up, elevator down." In other words, the economy and financial markets tend to grow and expand slowly but contract much more rapidly. As such, the road to business recovery is likely to take longer than it took to shut the economy down.

I hope I'm wrong.

But either way, you can use this book to help you plan out strategic cost-cutting. After all, even though companies often ignore rising costs and expenses in good times doesn't mean they should.

From a profitability standpoint, the best time to cut costs is any time at all.

Because whenever you cut costs, EBITDA rises.

Further Learning

If you've enjoyed this book and want to learn more about planning strategically for an uncertain future, I recommend the Certified Futurist and Long-Term Analyst™ — FLTA™ — training program that I created for The Futurist Institute. The FLTA™ trains analysts, consultants, executives, and professionals to incorporate trends into long-term strategic planning.

The FLTA™ has six distinct professional tracks, including consulting, national security, financial planning, accounting, legal, and standard tracks. Plus, The Futurist Institute is accredited by the Certified Financial Planner Board of Standards®, and the program includes 8.5 hours of CFP® continuing education hours. Other organizations also award hours for the FLTA™ program.

Details about the FLTA™ and The Futurist Institute are online at www.futuristinstitute.org.

Your Next Steps

The most important thing is to try and keep yourself and your loved ones out of harm's way. But the second most important thing is to keep your company out of harm's way — and cut costs!

Recovery will come. And if you look for opportunities to help your organization improve in the wake of this tragedy, you may be able to hasten the speed recovery.

Good luck and be well!
~ Jason Schenker
April 2020

COST-CUTTING TABLES

This section of the book includes three cost-cutting tables.

The first table is to list the top vendors by spend. The second table is to call out spend categories that are among "the usual suspects," where costs can be cut. The third table is for asset recovery, identification, repurposing, and disposition.

Vendor Name	Category	Spend
1.		
2.		
3.		
4.		
5.		
6.		
7.		
8.		
9.		
10.		

PRESTIGE ECONOMICS Top Vendors by Spend

Cost-Cutting
The Usual Suspects

Spend Categories	Total Spend	Potential Cuts
1. MRO		
2. Equipment		
3. Overtime		
4. Contracts		
5. Travel and Entertainment (T&E)		
Total Values		

PRESTIGE ECONOMICS

Asset Recovery
Identification and Repurpose/Disposition

Asset	Repurpose or Disposition	Disposition Value-add
1.		
2.		
3.		
4.		
5.		
	Total Value	

PRESTIGE ECONOMICS

ENDNOTES

Chapter 2

1. Definition of recession was retrieved on 12 April 2020 from http://www.nber.org/cycles.html.
2. "About the NBER" was retrieved on 12 April 2020 from http://www.nber.org/info.html.
3. This table was retrieved on 12 April 2020 from http://www.nber.org/cycles.html.

Chapter 6

1. Retrieved on 11 April 2020 from https://www.oecd.org/tax/crime/41353070.pdf.

ABOUT THE AUTHOR

Mr. Schenker is the President of Prestige Economics and Chairman of The Futurist Institute. He has been ranked one of the most accurate financial forecasters and futurists in the world. Bloomberg News has ranked Mr. Schenker a top forecaster in 43 categories, including #1 in the world for his accuracy in 25 categories, including for his forecasts of the Euro, the British Pound, the Russian Ruble, the Chinese RMB, crude oil prices, natural gas prices, gold prices, industrial metals prices, agricultural commodity prices, and U.S. jobs.

Mr. Schenker was ranked one of the top 100 most influential financial advisors in the world by Investopedia in 2018. His work has been featured in *The Wall Street Journal*, *The New York Times*, and the *Frankfurter Allgemeine Zeitung*. He has appeared on CNBC, CNN, ABC, NBC, MSNBC, Fox, Fox Business, BNN, Bloomberg Germany, and the BBC. Mr. Schenker has been a guest host of Bloomberg Television and he is a columnist for *Bloomberg Opinion*.

Mr. Schenker attends OPEC and Fed events, and he has given keynotes for private companies, public corporations, industry groups, and the U.S. Federal Reserve. He has advised NATO and the U.S. government on the future of work, blockchain, Bitcoin, cryptocurrency, quantum computing, data analysis, forecasting, and fake news. Mr. Schenker has written 24 books. Eleven have been #1 Best Sellers, including: *Jobs for Robots, Quantum: Computing Nouveau, Commodity Prices 101, Recession-Proof, Futureproof Supply Chain, Electing Recession, The Future of Finance is Now, The Future of Energy, The Dumpster Fire Election,* and *The Robot and Automation Almanac* for 2018 and 2020. Mr. Schenker also wrote *The Promise of Blockchain, Futureproof Supply Chain, The Fog of Data, Robot-Proof Yourself, Financial Risk Management Fundamentals, Midterm Economics, Spikes: Growth Hacking Leadership, Strategic Cost-Cutting, Reading the Economic Tea Leaves,* and *Be the Shredder, Not the Shred.* Mr. Schenker was featured as one of the world's foremost futurists in *After Shock.*

Mr. Schenker advises executives, industry groups, institutional investors, and central banks as the President of Prestige Economics. He also founded The Futurist Institute in October 2016, for which he created a rigorous course of study that includes *The Future of Work, The Future of Transportation, The Future of Data, The Future of Finance, Futurist Fundamentals, The Future of Energy, The Future of Leadership, The Future of Healthcare, and The Future of Quantum Computing.* Mr. Schenker is also an instructor for LinkedIn Learning courses on *Corporate Finance Risk Management, Audit and Due Diligence, Recession-Proof Strategies,* and a weekly *Economic Indicator* series. He has multiple other forthcoming LinkedIn Learning courses.

Mr. Schenker holds a Master's in Applied Economics from UNC Greensboro, a Master's in Negotiation, Conflict Resolution, and Peacebuilding from CSU Dominguez Hills, a Master's in Germanic Languages and Literature from UNC Chapel Hill, and a Bachelor's in History and German from The University of Virginia. He also holds a Certificate in FinTech from MIT, a Certificate in Supply Chain Management from MIT, a Certificate in Professional Development from UNC, a Certificate in Negotiation from Harvard Law School, a Certificate in Cybersecurity from Carnegie Mellon, and a Professional Certificate in Strategic Foresight from the University of Houston. Mr. Schenker holds the designations CMT® (Chartered Market Technician), ERP® (Energy Risk Professional), and CFP® (Certified Financial Planner). He is also a Certified Futurist and Long-Term Analyst™ and holds the FLTA™ designation.

Before founding Prestige Economics, Mr. Schenker worked as a Risk Specialist at McKinsey and Company, where he provided content direction to trading, risk, and commodity project teams on six continents. Prior to McKinsey, Mr. Schenker was the Chief Energy and Commodity Economist at Wachovia, which is now Wells Fargo. Based in Austin, Mr. Schenker is one of only 100 CEOs on the Texas Business Leadership Council, a non-partisan organization that advises Texas elected leadership at the state and federal level. Mr. Schenker is a Governance Fellow of the National Association of Corporate Directors. He also sits on multiple boards and is the VP of Finance on the Executive Committee of The Texas Lyceum, the preeminent non-partisan leadership group in Texas.

THE FUTURIST INSTITUTE

FI THE FUTURIST INSTITUTE

The Futurist Institute was founded in 2016 to help analysts, executives, and professionals incorporate new and emerging technology risk into their strategic planning. The Futurist Institute confers the Futurist and Long-Term Analyst™ (FLTA) designation and helps analysts become Certified Futurists™. Our courses have been approved for continuing education hours by the Certified Financial Planner Board of Standards (CFP Board), Global Association of Risk Professionals (GARP), and National Association of Certified Valuators and Analysts (NACVA).

Current Courses

The Future of Work
The Future of Data
The Future of Energy
The Future of Finance
The Future of Healthcare
The Future of Leadership
The Future of Transportation
Futurist Fundamentals
Quantum Computing

Visit The Futurist Institute:

www.futuristinstitute.org

PUBLISHER

Prestige Professional Publishing was founded in 2011 to produce insightful and timely professional reference books. We are registered with the Library of Congress.

Published Titles

Be the Shredder, Not the Shred
Commodity Prices 101
Electing Recession
Financial Risk Management Fundamentals
Futureproof Supply Chain
A Gentle Introduction to Audit and Due Diligence
Jobs for Robots
Midterm Economics
Quantum: Computing Nouveau
Reading the Economic Tea Leaves
Robot-Proof Yourself
Spikes: Growth Hacking Leadership
Strategic Cost-Cutting
The Dumpster Fire Election
The Fog of Data
The Future of Energy
The Future of Finance is Now
The Promise of Blockchain
The Robot and Automation Almanac — 2018
The Robot and Automation Almanac — 2019
The Robot and Automation Almanac — 2020

PUBLISHER

Forthcoming Titles

Content Monster
Disruption Warfare
The Future of Agriculture
The Future of Healthcare
The Future of Travel and Leisure

JOBS FOR ROBOTS

Jobs for Robots provides an in-depth look at the future of automation and robots, with a focus on the opportunities as well as the risks ahead. Job creation in coming years will be extremely strong for the kind of workers that do not require payroll taxes, healthcare, or vacation: robots. *Jobs for Robots* was published in February 2017. This book has been a #1 Best Seller on Amazon.

FINANCIAL RISK MANAGEMENT FUNDAMENTALS

Financial Risk Management Fundamentals examines nine different kinds of financial and non-financial risks in order to help corporate leaders identify, reduce, and mitigate them. The book was published in January 2019.

A GENTLE INTRODUCTION TO AUDIT AND DUE DILIGENCE

A Gentle Introduction to Audit and Due Diligence covers the critical basics and best practices of due diligence, internal audit, compilation, review, independent audit, and a number of other topics to prepare you to dig into financial data in a search for the truth. The book was published in December 2018.

DISCLAIMER

FROM THE AUTHOR

The following disclaimer applies to any content in this book:

This book is commentary intended for general information use only and is not investment advice. Jason Schenker does not make recommendations on any specific or general investments, investment types, asset classes, non-regulated markets, specific equities, bonds, or other investment vehicles. Jason Schenker does not guarantee the completeness or accuracy of analyses and statements in this book, nor does Jason Schenker assume any liability for any losses that may result from the reliance by any person or entity on this information. Opinions, forecasts, and information are subject to change without notice. This book does not represent a solicitation or offer of financial or advisory services or products; this book is only market commentary intended and written for general information use only. This book does not constitute investment advice. All links were correct and active at the time this book was published.

DISCLAIMER

FROM THE PUBLISHER

The following disclaimer applies to any content in this book:

This book is commentary intended for general information use only and is not investment advice. Prestige Professional Publishing, LLC does not make recommendations on any specific or general investments, investment types, asset classes, non-regulated markets, specific equities, bonds, or other investment vehicles. Prestige Professional Publishing, LLC does not guarantee the completeness or accuracy of analyses and statements in this book, nor does Prestige Professional Publishing, LLC assume any liability for any losses that may result from the reliance by any person or entity on this information. Opinions, forecasts, and information are subject to change without notice. This book does not represent a solicitation or offer of financial or advisory services or products; this book is only market commentary intended and written for general information use only. This book does not constitute investment advice. All links were correct and active at the time this book was published.

Prestige Professional Publishing, LLC

4412 City Park Road #4

Austin, Texas 78730

www.prestigeprofessionalpublishing.com

PRESTIGE
PROFESSIONAL PUBLISHING

ISBN: 978-1-946197-55-9 *Paperback*
978-1-946197-56-6 *Ebook*

Made in United States
Orlando, FL
04 November 2026

90202245R00105